100 THINGS
ARKANSAS FANS
SHOULD KNOW & DO
BEFORE THEY DIE

100 THINGS ARKANSAS FANS
SHOULD KNOW & DO
BEFORE THEY DIE

Rick Schaeffer

TRIUMPH
BOOKS

Library of Congress Cataloging-in-Publication Data

Schaeffer, Rick, 1950–
  100 things Arkansas fans should know & do before they die / Rick Schaeffer.
    pages cm
  ISBN 978-1-60078-991-5
  1. University of Arkansas, Fayetteville—Football—Miscellanea.
  2. Arkansas Razorbacks (Football team)—Miscellanea. 3. University of Arkansas, Fayetteville—Basketball—Miscellanea. 4. Arkansas Razorbacks (Basketball team)—Miscellanea. I. Title. II. Title: One hundred things Arkansas fans should know & do before they die.
  GV958.U515S35 2014
  796.332'630976714—dc23
                                        2014011275

This book is available in quantity at special discounts for your group or organization. For further information, contact:
  Triumph Books LLC
  814 North Franklin Street
  Chicago, Illinois 60610
  (312) 337-0747
  www.triumphbooks.com

Printed in U.S.A.
ISBN: 978-1-60078-991-5
Design by Patricia Frey
Photos courtesy of the Bob Cheyne family unless otherwise indicated

This book is dedicated to my wife, Adelaide, and my son, Benny, and his best friend Eddie, who is like a son, who graciously have surrendered time with me, so that Razorbacks fans may enjoy stories about their favorite coaches, players, broadcasters, and things to do.

This volume is also dedicated to the memory of Bob Cheyne, Arkansas' first sports information director, from 1948 to 1968. I spent two delightful hours with Bob, and his contributions to this work are significant. Five weeks later he passed away. We will miss him.

Contents

Foreword

When I arrived on the University of Arkansas campus as a freshman quarterback, I had my thoughts about how special this university could be. I also had notions about how special the people of this great state would be and how crazy and fanatical they would be. I was not disappointed.

The pride and passion of the people of Arkansas far exceeded my expectations. At the University of Arkansas, we have the most recognizable mascot in the entire country. Regardless of what city I am in, I smile with a sense of pride every time I see the Razorbacks logo.

Quick story: I was in the airport with my family, headed on vacation to the Bahamas. We saw a person walking through the airport with his family. He was wearing a Razorbacks hat and a Razorbacks shirt. We pointed at him and asked each other, "Did you see the Razorbacks fan?" Then, when we got to our destination in the Bahamas, we saw the same person and his family get on the shuttle bus that was headed to our resort. At that point, we struck up a conversation, and after a few minutes of talking Razorbacks football, you would have thought we'd been best friends forever.

We continued swapping Razorbacks stories, knowledge, and experiences, and before we knew it, a Hog Call broke out in the Bahamas—and we were proud to be part of it. That's the power of the Razorback. *100 Things Arkansas Fans Should Know & Do Before They Die* captures the great moments, stories, people, and things you should know and experience as a Hog fan that will continue to enhance your Razorbacks experience.

One of the things you should know about me is when I wake up every morning I'm proud to be a Razorback, and when I go to sleep at night I'm proud to be a Razorback. The choice I made to attend the University of Arkansas was one of the best decisions I've ever made. I thank my mother, Bobbye Grovey, and my father, Robert Grovey, for guiding me in the right direction. If I were a high school senior being recruited to play football again, I would choose Arkansas 10 out of 10 times, without hesitation.

When I committed to Coach Hatfield to play at the University, I referred to the eight-year Southwest Conference championship drought and told him I could lead the team to a championship if he hitched the wagon to me. I told him I wasn't coming to win games; I was coming to win championships. And win championships we did. I was very fortunate to play with great players and for great coaches who made it possible to win back-to-back SWC championships. In my opinion, we were one win away from playing for a national title in 1988. Needless to say, Coach Hatfield had a great impact on my life. I still consider him a mentor to this day.

After my playing career ended, I was blessed with the opportunity to work on the Razorback Sports Network as an analyst on Razorbacks football broadcasts. I'm so lucky to be a part of another fantastic team. Chuck Barrett, Scott Inman, Keith Jackson, and Rick Schaeffer are all incredible people. I can't tell you how *awesome* it is to show up each Saturday and describe Razorbacks football action to the most passionate fan base in the country. It's a privilege and an honor.

When preparing for a broadcast I sometimes find myself thinking about the moments when families are sitting around the radio, with no TV, listening to our broadcast. I think about the families who can't attend the game and are listening to us in their car because they are traveling to see a family member in need. I think about the hunters in the woods during deer season who are listening to our broadcast on their battery-powered radios. I think about all of the people who listen to our broadcast who couldn't wait for Paul Eells—and now, can't wait for Chuck Barrett—to say "Touchdown Arkansas!"

All of these things matter to me as a former player, and that's why I love being associated with this great university and this great state. The people of this great university and great state have enriched my life in so many ways. I have been so lucky to play quarterback at the University of Arkansas, to work for the Razorback Sports Network for 16 years and counting, to make my home in Arkansas, and to have married an Arkansas girl. All of these things have been true blessings to me, and have come because I made one of the best decisions of my life: to become a Razorback and attend the University of Arkansas.

Speaking of great people, the author of this book, Rick Schaeffer, is one of the finest people you will ever meet. I met Rick when I arrived on the UA campus as a freshman. The first thing that really stood out to me about him was how pleasant and nice he was to everyone. I thought to myself, *There's no possible way he can be that nice and respectful 24 hours a day.* Well, I'm here to tell you, 24 years later he still treats people the same way. He's really a great person and he shows respect for all people.

When it comes to Razorbacks history, Rick's knowledge is second to none. In preparation for our game broadcasts each week, I spend time watching film, reviewing notes, and analyzing stats. I usually come into the radio booth with a huge binder of information to help me break down the game. Rick strolls in with a flip card that shows the two-deep depth charts of the offense and defense. He reads the newspaper and he's ready.

Each week before we go on the air I watch to see if Rick will take any additional notes in preparation for the broadcast. He rarely does. That's because he's already mentally prepared for the broadcast. And when it is time for him to unleash his Razorbacks sports knowledge past or present, it's impressive to watch. Rick can describe a play from the 1960s and tell you which way Arkansas was moving down the field when the play happened, on what hash mark the ball was lined up, in what quarter of the game the play occurred, and how that game or play impacted the rest of the season.

The games, the players, the coaches, the winning plays, and the losing plays are embedded in his mind, and it is truly incredible to watch him unlock his mental vault. He is the Fort Knox of Razorbacks history. I'll admit that I'm occasionally guilty of using Rick as my personal Razorbacks Google search. Most of the time it's just easier for me to ask him instead of firing up my computer and going online to find the answer.

With this book, he can be your personal Razorbacks expert, too. Rick Schaeffer is a true historian regarding Razorbacks athletics, and with this book he will educate you and point you in the right direction when creating your Razorbacks fan bucket list. Enjoy!

—Quinn Grovey

Introduction

During my 24 years in the sports information office at the University of Arkansas, it was my pleasure to serve hundreds of coaches and thousands of student-athletes who brought favorable attention to the school through their efforts as Razorbacks. It was a privilege to work with each and every one of them. They all had one common denominator: they competed fiercely because they so appreciated the support they were given by the fantastic fan base. Those fans take enormous pride in the accomplishments of the Razorbacks.

The only aspect of this book I regret is not being able to mention them all. Every person who put on a Razorbacks uniform in any sport deserves recognition, but this publication is limited to fewer than 100. Perhaps there will be immediate demand for a sequel.

There are obvious choices. The first three begin with B: Bezdek, Barnhill, and Broyles. Hugo Bezdek was the first big-time football coach at Arkansas, and it was his quote, that his team played "like a wild band of razorback hogs," that led to a mascot change. John Barnhill was the football coach and athletic director who understood the importance of uniting the state of Arkansas behind one program. Frank Broyles was not only the winningest football coach in school history but also served as athletic director for more than three decades, giving him a combined 50 years as the best-known Razorback.

It was easy to pick other athletes and coaches with whom most Razorbacks fans would be familiar. And there are some inclusions in this book that will cause debate as to whether another person or event was more worthy. Stimulating conversation is a good thing.

All of us have personal memories that are important to us. I grew up in Oklahoma but loved the hogs on the Arkansas helmets and became a Razorbacks fan. My first memory is of watching the 1961 Cotton Bowl on television (before the hogs were on the helmets) and seeing Lance Alworth return a punt against Duke. Unfortunately the Razorbacks missed the extra point and lost 7–6.

I remember watching the Sugar Bowl games against Alabama and Mississippi on television following the 1961 and '62 seasons. I was very young but still impressionable. I didn't watch every play like I do now but can still remember seeing the images on a black-and-white television.

In 1964 I loved listening to the radio. Indeed, '60s music still resonates with me. On Saturday nights I would tune into 50,000-watt KAAY and listen to the Razorbacks games. I can still remember Bob Cheyne describing Texas' failed two-point conversion attempt that allowed Arkansas to escape with a 14–13 win at Austin in 1964. And I watched the Cotton Bowl on television that New Year's Day when the Razorbacks earned a national championship with a victory over Nebraska.

I worked for a florist in Oklahoma City who allowed me to watch Arkansas' victory over Georgia in the 1969 Sugar Bowl on his color television. Not many of us had color televisions back then. I was a freshman at Oklahoma State and lived and died with every play watching the 1969 Arkansas-Texas shootout. To this day, I still can't watch the fourth quarter.

In 1971 I bought Cotton Bowl tickets expecting Arkansas to be there after the Razorbacks beat Texas in Little Rock. Like other Hogs fans, I was disappointed that a tie with Rice knocked Arkansas out of the Cotton Bowl's host spot.

In 1975 I again bought tickets to the Cotton Bowl, after the Razorbacks beat Texas A&M. I can remember almost every play of the Hogs' victory over Georgia. By the next fall I was a Razorback for good, joining Butch Henry in the sports information office. The first athlete I met was Ron Calcagni. The first freshman class I worked with included Houston Nutt and Robert Farrell, a legendary pass-catch combo from Little Rock Central.

A banquet capped a day of celebration for the 1964 national champion Razorbacks.

At that time the assistant sports information director traveled with the basketball team and I immediately became the color analyst on road games. Eddie Sutton allowed me to listen to the pregame scouting reports, which enabled me to sound a lot smarter than I was. Even after becoming sports information director, I traveled with the football and basketball teams and did color on both broadcasts until leaving the department at the end of July 2000.

I was able to remain on the UA baseball broadcasts since Chuck Barrett's arrangement with his network when he went statewide with his radio show prohibited him from doing the midweek games. A couple years later Todd Curtis asked if I would be interested in coming back to the basketball broadcasts. Then it was back to football, first doing stats for Paul Eells, then Mike Nail for a year, and then Chuck. When the pregame expanded to an hour and a half, I had the privilege of joining Quinn Grovey and Scott Inman for that program.

I still love the hog on the helmet—or the shorts or jerseys or whatever a particular team is wearing. And it is a privilege to share these stories with you. Many include personal observations but all are through the eyes of the participants. Enjoy debating what should or should not have been included, but most of all, enjoy the stories themselves.

1 Frank Broyles

After a standout career in three sports at Georgia Tech interrupted by a brief time in the military during World War II, Frank Broyles became an assistant football coach at Baylor at age 22. He hoped to become a head coach by the time he was 30 and he was looking for a school that didn't have to fight an in-state rival for support.

He found just what he was looking for in Fayetteville, Arkansas. At the time of his first visit, Fayetteville was a tiny hamlet nestled into the foothills of the Ozarks. Yet even as a Baylor assistant coach he couldn't help but notice Razorbacks everywhere when the Bears visited for their Southwest Conference football game.

"I grew up in Georgia and there was fierce rivalry between Georgia and Georgia Tech," said Broyles. "Georgia got most of the good football players because Georgia Tech was limited to students who wanted to major in engineering. That changed later.

"The first time I was in Arkansas I thought how wonderful it would be to coach somewhere that enjoyed the support of the entire state. From that point on, Arkansas was the job I truly wanted."

Broyles later moved back to his alma mater, Georgia Tech, as an assistant coach. He was on the staff when the Yellow Jackets met Arkansas in the 1955 Cotton Bowl. He got to know UA athletic director John Barnhill at events surrounding the game, and when Coach Bowden Wyatt left the Hogs for Tennessee shortly after the Cotton Bowl, Broyles told Barnhill he would love the job.

Barnhill liked Broyles but wasn't interested in hiring the young coach; his policy was to hire head coaches only. He felt Arkansas was prestigious enough to lure a coach who already had been

1

successful in directing a program. Broyles was disappointed but didn't give up his dream of coaching the Razorbacks.

Broyles' first head coaching job came at Missouri. He directed the Tigers in 1957 and planned to stay in Columbia for a while. But, after the season, Jack Mitchell, the coach hired by Barnhill when Wyatt left, decided to leave Arkansas to become head coach at Kansas. This time Barnhill called Broyles. Famously, Broyles quipped, "Barney, what took you so long?"

The Razorbacks lost their first six games in 1958 and Broyles wondered if he had made a good decision. Arkansas fans might have been wondering if Broyles was the right man for the job. Fortunately for the young Georgia Tech grad, the Hogs won their last four.

The winning had just begun. Arkansas won or shared Southwest Conference titles in each of the next three seasons. During an era when there weren't many bowl games, the Hogs visited the Gator Bowl, the Cotton Bowl, and the Sugar Bowl twice in a four-year period.

After a disappointing 5–5 season in 1963, the Hogs went undefeated in 1964 and earned the post-bowl version of the national championship by beating Nebraska in the Cotton Bowl. The Razorbacks were 10–0 in 1965, stretching their school-record winning streak to 22 before falling to LSU in the Cotton Bowl at season's end.

Broyles' team closed the decade strong with a 28–5 record from 1968–70, including two more trips to the Sugar Bowl. His last great hurrah as a coach came in 1975, when the Razorbacks stunned second ranked Texas A&M 31–6 in the regular-season finale and earned a trip to the Cotton Bowl. Arkansas thumped SWC co-champion Georgia 31–10 in the Cotton Bowl to finish the season 10–2.

Early in the 1976 season, Broyles decided it would be his last as coach. He and close friend and coaching rival Darrell Royal each coached their last game against each other in a regular-season finale that had been earmarked for television long before the season began.

In 1973 Broyles had added the title of athletic director. (It was not uncommon during that time for one man to be both head football coach and athletic director. Bear Bryant at Alabama and Royal at Texas were among those who held both positions.) After Broyles coached his last game, he remained as athletic director. His strong leadership produced an all-sports program with facilities that late in his tenure were ranked best in the SEC.

Broyles was responsible for three expansions of Razorback Stadium; the renovation of Barnhill Arena; construction of Bud Walton Arena, Baum Stadium, the John McDonnell Outdoor Track, the Tyson Indoor Track Center, the George Billingsley Tennis Center, the Broyles Athletic Center, and the Pat and Willard Walker Indoor Workout Facility and Weight Room; and brokered an agreement for the Hogs golf team to play at the Blessings.

He hired only two basketball coaches during his first 28 years as athletic director: Eddie Sutton and Nolan Richardson, and both men took Razorbacks basketball to never-before-experienced success, including a national championship under Richardson. Broyles hired just one track coach, John McDonnell, who earned the greatest record of any coach in the history of the NCAA by guiding the Razorbacks indoor track, outdoor track, and cross country teams to a combined 40 national championships. His only two hires in baseball, Norm DeBriyn and Dave Van Horn, both took the Hogs to the College World Series.

Broyles said Arkansas was "the only job I ever wanted. Everywhere I went I told people what a privilege it was for me to be at Arkansas. It was 50 years of absolutely loving my job." A member of the College Football Hall of Fame for his coaching achievements, Broyles' last day as AD was December 31, 2007. It was the completion of 50 years on the job. A statue of Broyles now graces the entry into the Broyles Athletic Center, the complex that housed UA football coaches from 1975 through 2012 and still offices the current administrative staff.

2 Hugo Bezdek

While Arkansas fielded its first football team in 1894, the program resembled little more than a club sport before Hugo Bezdek was hired as head coach before the 1908 season. Before him, seven different faculty members had rotated as coach in the program's first 14 seasons, and the first seven teams played no more than five games in a year.

Bezdek, born in Prague, was a fullback at the University of Chicago, where he earned his degree. He went on to serve as head football coach at Oregon for a year before moving to Arkansas, where he took on the double assignment of football and baseball head. After an initial 5–4 gridiron campaign, Bezdek discovered Steve Creekmore playing intramurals.

Creekmore became Bezdek's quarterback for the next two seasons and Arkansas went 7–0 in 1909 and 7–1 in 1910. Then known as the Cardinals, Arkansas beat LSU 16–0 and Ouachita Baptist 55-0 on a two-game road swing to win the unofficial Championship of the South in 1909. The distinction was a big deal at a time when there were no polls, bowls, or even an NCAA.

Bezdek is given credit for Arkansas' official mascot name change. He described his 1909 team as "a wild band of razorback hogs." In five years, Bezdek compiled a record of 29–13–1. His

Steve Creekmore quarterbacked Arkansas' undefeated football team in 1909.

Why Otis Douglas?

Of all the football coaching hires made through the years, the one that makes the least sense was Otis Douglas. John Barnhill had revived the program from 1946 to 1949, but was suffering from health problems. As athletic director, it was his task to replace himself as head coach going into the 1950 season. Douglas was then an assistant coach with the Philadelphia Eagles, who were winning big in the NFL. Barnhill listened to fans complaints that the Hogs did not have a "pro" attack. With that in mind, he hired Douglas knowing the decision would either be brilliant or awful.

As it turned out, it was awful. Douglas assumed the players were adults and treated them as he did the pro players in his charge. Discipline among players was practically nonexistent. In his book *The Razorbacks*, Orville Henry quoted Fred Williams, who would go on to star for the Chicago Bears, as saying, "We didn't win many games but we didn't lose any parties." Arkansas finished 2–8, 5–5, and 2–8 in Douglas' campaigns. None of those teams won a game in the state of Texas, a rather essential element in competing in the SWC since all of the schools except Arkansas were in Texas. Many of his players, including Williams, Dave "Hog" Hanner, Pat Summerall, Lamar McHan, Lew Carpenter, and Bob Griffin, went on to long NFL careers. Unfortunately, Douglas was not able to win much with those players while he was at Arkansas.

winning percentage of .686 stood as the best in Arkansas history until Frank Broyles eclipsed it during his 19-year career.

Bezdek wasn't yet 30 when he left Arkansas to return to the University Oregon as head football and baseball coach. He remained there through the 1917 season, then served as head football coach at Penn State for a dozen years.

In those days, the Major League Baseball season ended before the college football season began, and there was little for a college football coach to do between regular seasons. So Bezdek took on quite a summer job in managing the Pittsburgh Pirates during the 1917, 1918, and 1919 seasons before returning to his college football teams in the fall.

At Penn State, his teams were always successful. Indeed, his Nittany Lions advanced to the Rose Bowl when it was the only postseason contest in college football.

Believe it or not, Bezdek holds even more coaching distinctions. He was the first coach of the Cleveland Rams when they entered the National Football League in 1937. He continued to coach through the first three games of the 1938 campaign as well, but compiled a miserable record of 1-13.

His NFL career may have been ignominious, but his accomplishments on the collegiate level earned Bezdek a spot in the College Football Hall of Fame.

John Barnhill

A guard at Tennessee in the late 1920s, John Barnhill was an assistant coach at his alma mater for 10 seasons before the Volunteers' legendary coach, General Robert Neyland, left the program to serve in World War II. Barnhill was named interim head coach in Neyland's absence, which spanned the entire war. In five seasons, Barnhill compiled a record of 32–5–2, good enough for nearly any coach to keep his job. However, Barnhill wasn't in a typical position. When Neyland returned to Knoxville, the old coach took the reins again.

Arkansas was quick to nab Barnhill as head football coach when he became available. Barnhill recognized the power of being in a state with just one major program and pioneered significant moves that are still being used today. First, he knew many of Arkansas' best college football prospects were leaving the state. And who could blame them? The Razorbacks had posted just one winning record in the nine years before Barnhill arrived. He became determined to keep the best players in state by building statewide support. When Clyde Scott, who could have gone anywhere after leaving the military at the conclusion of the war, joined Barnhill at Arkansas, it was a significant step toward making the Razorbacks attractive for in-state players.

In his effort to build statewide support, Barnhill declared the Razorbacks would not play any other in-state schools—in any sport. The Hogs had played Arkansas A&M in football as recently as 1944, but Barnhill's declaration has stood the test of time. The University of Arkansas hasn't played a football game against anyone else from within the state's borders since.

"John Barnhill realized that most of Arkansas' limited resources would be needed to have a great football program," said Frank Broyles. "It was vital to have the support of the entire state. He did everything he could to unite the people in every corner of our state behind the Razorbacks."

Barnhill also recognized the impact radio could have on his program and initiated the idea, later enhanced by Broyles, of giving game broadcasts free of charge to any stations in Arkansas that would carry them. That effort pretty much eliminated competition from broadcasts of LSU, Oklahoma, Ole Miss, and others. And since this was long before the days of college football on television, Barnhill was able to dominate the football landscape for his Razorbacks.

Scott had a sensational season as running back and safety, and Barnhill's first team won the Southwest Conference championship and met national power LSU in the Cotton Bowl. Despite making just one first down on a field frozen by an overnight ice storm, Arkansas held back the Tigers for a 0–0 tie.

Barnhill's second team won six games, including a victory over William and Mary in the Dixie Bowl, but the Hogs finished just 5-5 in the next two seasons with an injured Scott on the bench.

After being diagnosed with multiple sclerosis after the 1949 campaign, Barnhill stepped down as head football coach but remained as athletic director. He stayed in that spot until 1970. His most notable hire, of course, was Broyles, whom he secured as football coach in December 1957.

"We were a very poor state, but John Barnhill could write a letter to our top 100 financial supporters and get more aid from those 100 than anyone I've ever known," said former sports information director Bob Cheyne. "He got facilities because people believed in him. He did everything for the University of Arkansas, not for John Barnhill. He never promoted himself."

Broyles greatly admired Barnhill and kept most of his policies intact. In addition, the two formed a personal relationship. Broyles noted, "Barney lived in Fayetteville until he died. I consulted with him frequently after he retired."

When Arkansas built a new facility for basketball in the mid-1950s, the school named it after its athletic director. Cheyne said, "Barney never would have wanted the field house named after him but members of the athletic council insisted. A professor of biology who knew Barnhill well knew Barnhill was the reason we would have that field house."

After renovations came Eddie Sutton, then Nolan Richardson, who coached the basketball Razorbacks, and Barnhill Arena became one of the most feared places in the country for visiting teams. Today, the facility is used for volleyball and gymnastics.

4 Cardinals to Razorbacks

During the Civil War, troops from Arkansas were frequently referred to as "Razorbacks" in reference to the wild boars that were plentiful in the state at that time. The term was a familiar one, already linked to the state. However, when the University of Arkansas started a football program in 1894, it chose "Cardinals" as the school nickname. The school color was heliotrope, a shade of purple.

Hired as head football coach in 1908 at the ridiculously young age of 24, Hugo Bezdek frequently compared his team to razorbacks because of the way they fought and clawed to the very end of every game. Students liked the term, and adopted Razorbacks a second nickname. In Bezdek's mind the mascot already had changed. After all, he figured, razorbacks were much more tenacious than cardinals.

Late in the 1909 season, after Arkansas won two games on a road trip, Bezdek and his players were greeted with great enthusiasm by students and other fans when their train rolled into the station at Fayetteville. One of the wins on the two-game road swing was over LSU, already recognized as a regional powerhouse. It was a happy scene. In their first 15 years, Arkansas football teams had won more than four games only once. The 1909 squad was different; it ultimately finished 7–0 and was recognized as unofficial "Champion of the South," a very prestigious title at the time.

Steve Creekmore, who quarterbacked Arkansas to a combined record of 14-1 in 1909–10, said years later that his team used an early version of the hurry-up offense. There was no such thing as the huddle in football during those years, but Arkansas operated at a fast pace. Its players would line up and snap the ball as soon as the official set it ready for play.

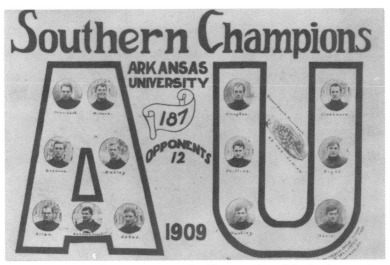

Arkansas' undefeated 1909 team won the Championship of the South.

Creekmore said, "I guess it was a forerunner of Oklahoma's hurry-up style in the split-T days under Bud Wilkinson. The LSU coach protested our system, but it was legal."

Collegiate sports were much more regional then. And going undefeated by beating teams like LSU and Oklahoma was a big deal. So when the Arkansas team arrived at the Fayetteville train station in 1909 after defeating LSU, Bezdek took the opportunity to address the crowd. He invoked his favorite simile: that his team played "like a wild band of Razorback hogs." Students and fans loved it.

However, making the official designation took time. The school yearbook was still *The Cardinal* as late as 1912. Then in 1913, it became *The Razorback*. At some point the school colors changed, too. They became cardinal and white. Though the changeover can be marked, there is no official record of the circumstances.

Surely it was Bezdek who hastened the change. He also coached Arkansas' baseball teams during his five-year tenure at the school, and team pictures—even before 1913—show the players wearing uniforms with a razorback depicted on the front. Bezdek had it figured out.

While the razorback hog is now extinct in Arkansas, there are plenty of the animal's close relatives left. The university uses a Russian boar as its mascot today and it is impossible for most to tell the difference between it and the razorback that is now just a legend in Arkansas.

Since that day in 1909, millions of UA fans have "called the Hogs" in cheering on the Razorbacks. Arkansas is the only college in the United States to have a Razorback as its mascot.

5 1964 Football National Champions

Any national football championship awarded in college football's earliest decades was mythical. Then in 1936, the Associated Press started its weekly poll. That led to the crowning of a national champion at the end of the regular season.

Later, bowl games were considered a nice reward for the few teams that earned the limited spots available in the 1950s and early 1960s, but those postseason results were not taken into account by AP or its competitor, United Press International.

Even an unbeaten season was no guarantee for a No. 1 spot in the final polls. And when Arkansas went 10–0 in 1964, the Hogs were ranked number two in the final AP poll, behind Alabama, whose record was also 10–0.

Arkansas' run to a perfect record was spearheaded by a defense that shut out its last five opponents. After hard-fought victories over Oklahoma State and University of Tulsa to open the season,

Members of the 1964 UA national championship team pose in front of Wilson Sharp, the athletic dorm at the time.

the Razorbacks breezed past TCU and Baylor to set up their annual showdown with Texas.

The Longhorns had won the 1963 national title and were ranked No. 1 again in 1964. However, despite Texas' past success against Arkansas (and just about everyone else), UA coach Frank Broyles always had the Hogs ready to play the 'Horns. In fact, in 1960 Arkansas won at Austin with a late field goal; and only a disputed fumble and late Longhorns touchdown march allowed Texas to prevail, again at home, in 1962.

Arkansas' 1964 defense was stout and the Razorbacks had the nation's top punt returner in Ken Hatfield. Texas coach Darrell Royal assured reporters before the game, "Hatfield won't have any long punt returns against us." But Hatfield proved Royal wrong. His 81-yard punt return for a touchdown was the first score of the game—and it remains one of the most significant plays in Arkansas history.

"When I caught the ball at our 19, I knew they had kicked it too far, and I knew we could block them," Hatfield said. "Jim Lindsey threw the first block. When I went to the wall on the sideline our whole team was there. Our players knocked down eight of them."

Buy Land

Jim Lindsey came along at the right time. Lindsey was an inspirational leader of the Hogs during their 22-game winning streak that ended in his last game, a 14–7 loss to LSU in the 1966 Cotton Bowl. He made several big plays but did not produce extraordinary numbers.

When he finished his Razorbacks career at the end of that 1965 season, the NFL and AFL had not yet combined and still bid against each other for football players in dueling drafts. It was the Minnesota Vikings that convinced him to go to the NFL. It ended up being a wise decision. He played seven years in Minnesota for excellent teams, one of which made it to the Super Bowl. He was highly influenced by head coach Bud Grant but also still valued the input of Frank Broyles and E.J. Ball, a lawyer in Fayetteville.

Lindsey was considering what to do with his bonus money and other NFL earnings when Broyles and Ball both urged him to buy land in northwest Arkansas. So, that's what he did. He purchased plenty of land, including several acres on a hill that was on the northern edge of Fayetteville. "My father told me it was the stupidest thing I ever had done," said Lindsey, "but I bought it anyway." It turned out to be a pretty smart buy. A few years later he sold it for an enormous profit— it had been selected as the best place to build the Northwest Arkansas Mall. Broyles and Ball had the vision, and Lindsey had the funds to make what turned out to be a very good investment.

The punt return did not totally deflate Texas. It took a late stand on a Longhorns two-point conversion try to finally secure the victory. After scoring a touchdown to slice Arkansas' advantage to 14–13, Royal wanted to take his chances for the win.

"Their substitution caused us to think they would pass rather than run," said Hatfield. "We changed to a wider defense. Sure enough, their quarterback tried to throw a pass in the flat but Jim Fitch was rushing the passer, got in his face, and made him throw low. With so little time left, we knew the game was over."

Coach Royal, who was great friends with Broyles, came to the Arkansas locker room to congratulate the Hogs, telling them, "You beat a great Texas team. We won't lose again. If you let up at all we will catch you."

Arkansas won its last five games, shutting out Wichita State, Texas A&M, Rice, SMU, and Texas Tech. Texas won its last five as well. The Razorbacks earned the Southwest Conference's host spot in the Cotton Bowl against a 9–1 Nebraska team. Texas was invited to the Orange Bowl to play top-ranked Alabama.

Arkansas' light, quick, swarming defenders somehow slowed Nebraska's power running attack. When Bobby Burnett scored a late touchdown on a sweep around end, the Hogs managed a 10–7 victory. That evening, the Razorbacks turned their attention to the Orange Bowl. Royal kept his promise. The Longhorns won once more, squeezing past the Crimson Tide.

"After we celebrated the victory over Nebraska, we all watched the Orange Bowl on television," said Hatfield. "It's rare that we would pull for Texas, but we did that night. When they upset Alabama, we knew we were national champions."

At the time, of the major groups, only the Football Writers of America awarded a national championship that took the postseason into consideration. Unsurprisingly, Arkansas was the winner, and a championship presentation was scheduled in Fayetteville.

Because of what happened in the Orange Bowl on January 1, 1965, the Associated Press changed its policy. Beginning after the following season, it waited until after the bowl games to name its national champion. UPI didn't follow suit until 1971. Today it would be unimaginable to pick the No. 1 team based on the regular season alone. That's why Arkansas isn't bashful at all about claiming the 1964 national title.

1994 Basketball National Champions

As freshmen, Corliss Williamson and Scotty Thurman helped lead Arkansas deep into the 1993 NCAA Men's Basketball Tournament. The Hogs beat Holy Cross and St. John's at Winston Salem, North Carolina, to earn a spot opposite the University of North Carolina in the Sweet Sixteen at the Meadowlands in East Rutherford, New Jersey.

The Todd Day–Lee Mayberry–Oliver Miller era had ended a season earlier, and Darrell Hawkins and Robert Shepherd were the only seniors on the '93 Razorbacks. Williamson and Thurman, along with sophomore transfers Corey Beck and Dwight Stewart and sophomore Clint McDaniel, were the ringleaders of the next wave of Arkansas success.

The 1993 Hogs were fiercely competitive, but lacked the size necessary to go deeper in the tournament. North Carolina nearly matched Arkansas' quickness—and had a towering height advantage. Nonetheless, the Hogs stayed in it until the end, when their season ended with an 80–74 heartbreaker against the eventual national champion Tar Heels.

Gracing the Cover

What do Harry Jones, Ron Calcagni, Ben Cowins, Lou Holtz, Sidney Moncrief, Corliss Williamson, Corey Beck, and former President Bill Clinton have in common? They've all been on the cover of *Sports Illustrated* representing the Razorbacks. Jones appeared in 1965 as the inside article chronicled Arkansas as "the New Dynasty." Calcagni, Cowins, and Holtz graced the cover of the 1978 college football preview as *SI* ranked the Razorbacks No. 1. Moncrief's cover shot in 1978 was one of *SI*'s all-time bests—Sidney was caught in full flight in a dunk against Texas. Clinton was adorned in Razorbacks sweats during the 1994 season and Williamson was on the cover after the Hogs won the '94 national title. Beck made the cover in 1995 when the Razorbacks earned a return spot in the Final Four.

When freshmen Darnell Robinson and Lee Wilson, both 6'11", were added in 1994, the Razorbacks had secured the size they needed to go all the way.

It was a charmed year. The Razorbacks moved into Bud Walton Arena, a 19,200-seat palace that more than doubled the capacity of their previous home, Barnhill Arena. The Hogs were 16–0 at home and ranked fourth nationally in attendance with an average of more than 20,000 per game. Every Bud Walton win was by at least 10 points except a one-point triumph over LSU.

Arkansas was just as tough on the road, winning eight of its 10 away games. The Hogs were 24-2 entering the SEC Tournament at Memphis. After beating Georgia, the Razorbacks lost to Kentucky—but that didn't keep them from being a No. 1 seed.

"It had been a great year up to that point," said Thurman. "That first year in Bud Walton was amazing. Barnhill had been a great place to play in but Bud Walton was more than twice as big. We knew we had a good team and we thought we could win it all. We gained a lot of confidence from the NCAA Tournament the year before. We all thought we should have beaten North Carolina."

Thurman and Williamson had been the bell cows to that point. Williamson averaged more 20 points per game and Thurman gave the Hogs wins with last second shots at Tennessee and LSU. Beck and McDaniel were the best defensive guards in the country, and Alex Dillard came off the bench firing and making three-pointers from extra-long distances.

Arkansas' first three NCAA tourney wins came easily against North Carolina A&T, Georgetown, and Tulsa. In the regional finals, with President (and former Arkansas governor) Bill Clinton watching, Thurman scored 20 points to lead the Hogs past Michigan, which still featured four of the original "Fab Five."

The Final Four was played in Charlotte, North Carolina. Even though the Razorbacks had been ranked No. 1 for nine weeks during the 1994 season, had won the SEC regular-season title, and were making their second Final Four appearance in five years under coach Nolan Richardson's direction, Richardson convinced his team that they were still considered underdogs by the national audience.

"Nolan used the no-respect motivation to the hilt," legendary sportswriter Orville Henry said at the time. "He had his players thinking they were significant underdogs. He told his team that the national media thought Arizona's guards were the best in the country and that Arkansas couldn't stop them."

Damon Stoudamire and Khalid Reeves were spectacular, no doubt. But in the semifinal game, they struggled with the tenacious defense of Beck and McDaniel. The pair hit just 11 of their 43 shots. Williamson had 29 points for the Razorbacks and Arkansas advanced with a 91–82 victory.

Henry noted, "Nolan used the media in the championship game, too. When it was suggested Duke's players were highly intelligent and Arkansas won with athleticism, Nolan told his players the media thought the Razorbacks were dumb. He jumped on media members for that at the pre–championship game press conference."

Things didn't look good for the Hogs early in the second half when Duke jumped to a 10-point lead, but after a Richardson timeout, the Razorbacks countered with an 8–0 blitz that made it tight again. Arkansas led 70–65 late in the game but the Blue Devils tied it with 1:29 remaining.

While the Hogs normally had a quick trigger on offense, the next possession bled the shot clock. In fact, Thurman almost didn't get off the most famous shot in UA history.

"The shot clock was winding down when Dwight Stewart took a pass at the top of the circle," Thurman recalled. "He was going to shoot but he fumbled the ball. So, he passed to me and I put it up."

Thurman's shot left his hand just before the shot clock clicked to zero. It was a high archer, just over the outstretched hand of a defender, and settled into the cylinder with less than a minute left. Duke never recovered, and Arkansas had won the national championship.

"I had the privilege of making a lot of great calls during my 29 years of broadcasting Razorback basketball, but winning the national championship stood out," said long time basketball announcer and "Voice of the Razorbacks" Mike Nail.

Thurman added, "People have reminded me of that shot nearly every day of my life even though it was 20 years ago."

President Clinton came to the floor and congratulated Richardson. He later had the opportunity to congratulate the entire team in a Rose Garden ceremony at the White House.

Nolan Richardson

Nolan Richardson took a difficult path to becoming the winningest basketball coach in Razorbacks history as well as the author of Arkansas' 1994 national championship campaign. He left the very successful program he had built at Tulsa to become the first African-American basketball coach in UA and Southwest Conference history. At the time he was hired, he was one of only six African-American head coaches out of over 300 division one schools.

His first few years were tumultuous. Richardson inherited a program that had been to the NCAA Tournament nine consecutive years, including one trip to the Final Four, under the direction of coach Eddie Sutton. Richardson's fast-paced style was a stark contrast to the Sutton era. And when his first team finished with a losing record and his second played in the NIT, Richardson was subject to criticism from Hogs fans who weren't sure the style change was worth it.

Richardson also suffered from personal struggles early on. During his second year at Arkansas, Richardson and his wife, Rose, lost their daughter, Yvonne, to leukemia. They were devastated. However, Nolan returned to coach the Hogs after his daughter's death, and began to engineer Arkansas' rise to a spot among the national elite.

By the time the 1989–90 season began, it became clear that Richardson had built a powerhouse. Led by sophomores Todd Day, Lee Mayberry, and Oliver Miller, the Razorbacks reached the Final Four. That season launched a six-year period during which Arkansas won more games than any team in the country. The Hogs reached the Elite Eight in 1991, the Sweet Sixteen in 1993, won

Nolan Walks Out

Nolan Richardson told his team he would never see them lose to Texas in the Super Drum on the UT campus. So, with his team trailing by three points with only seconds left and one of Texas' best players, Lance Blanks, at the foul line shooting one and one, what was Nolan to do? He decided to take a stroll. He headed for the dressing room. At first no one knew what to do. Finally, the play continued. "We thought he was upset about the officiating," said Lee Mayberry. "He was probably like everyone in the building and thought Lance would make the free throws. He was a good free throw shooter. But we knew that if he missed we still had a chance." Sure enough, Blanks missed. The Hogs rebounded and got the ball to Mayberry. He swished a 30-footer with three seconds left to send the game into overtime.

"I wanted to take that shot," Mayberry said. 'We had a lot of guys who could have made it but I was still upset about an intentional foul they had called on me and I wanted to take the shot." Nolan came back for the overtime and the Razorbacks dominated the extra session, eventually winning by eight points.

the national title in 1994, advanced to the championship game again in 1995, and were in the Sweet Sixteen again in 1996. It was the greatest period in the history of Arkansas basketball.

What was it like to play for him? "Tough but rewarding," said Scotty Thurman, a standout on the 1993–95 teams. "He demanded a lot of you. When you are 18, 19 years old, it doesn't register, but looking back I realize why he was so demanding. He was like a father figure to me and a lot like my own father. He had a unique sense of humor and commanding presence.

"He used to tell us, the harder I work, the luckier I get. He scheduled six AM practices, which we thought were crazy. Now, if I wake up after six, I feel like I've missed something. Getting up early stuck with me. We all felt like family."

Richardson's teams won with tenacious full-court pressure and a fast-paced offense that produced plenty of high-scoring games. His teams scored 100 or more points 99 times, and of the top 34 point totals in school history, all but one occurred with Richardson as coach. In fact, Arkansas had scored 100 or more points in a game just 29 times before Richardson's arrival.

His overall record was 390–170 in 17 seasons. His teams won Southwest Conference regular-season and tournament championships in each of their last three seasons in the league and earned the Southeastern Conference regular-season title in their initial campaign in that league. From 1990 to 1995, Arkansas won 175 games and was 21–5 in NCAA Tournament games.

Richardson's teams filled Barnhill Arena, then Bud Walton Arena, to the rafters during the late 1980s and throughout the '90s. He brought great pride to Razorbacks fans as his teams beat the best of the best. Arkansas defeated Duke twice, once for the national championship. The Hogs twice beat North Carolina in the NCAA Tournament. Richardson's teams beat Kentucky in the regular season in each of Arkansas' first four years in the SEC. The Hogs also beat basketball powerhouses Michigan, Arizona, Syracuse, Georgetown, St. John's, Memphis, and Marquette along with every team in the SWC and SEC during their amazing Richardson-led run.

"Nolan Richardson made Arkansas basketball cool," said former ESPN college basketball analyst Jimmy Dykes, who now coaches the UA women's basketball team. "That was very important at the time. UNLV, Kentucky, Louisville, Georgetown, and Duke were the 'it' teams of that era, and Arkansas jumped right into the middle of the pack. That is not easy to do.

"Arkansas dominated in Barnhill Arena, then at Bud Walton Arena. In the two years the Razorbacks were in the SEC and played in Barnhill, they played 16 games at Barnhill and averaged 94.7 points in those games. They were dominant. They had a different style, look, and feel. If you were involved in college basketball, you had to sit up and pay attention to what Nolan Richardson was doing at Arkansas."

Richardson's tenure of 17 years was the longest consecutive tenure in team history. (Glen Rose actually coached the Hogs for 23 seasons, but he was at Arkansas nine years, left and came back later for 14 more seasons. Despite that, Richardson's teams still won 65 more games than Rose's.)

The Greatest Decade

Frank Broyles was beginning his third season as Arkansas' head football coach in 1960 as a new decade of college football was launched. By the end of the decade, the Razorbacks would be regarded as a national power and Broyles would be recognized as one of the nation's top coaches. During his tenure, Arkansas won the post-bowl versions of the 1964 national championship when the Razorbacks were the only unbeaten team (11–0) still standing after all the bowl games were over.

Amazingly, the Hogs came close to winning three other national titles. In 1962, Arkansas' only regular-season loss was to Texas at Austin. A controversial fumble into the Longhorns end zone (the Razorbacks thought Danny Brabham had cleared the goal line before the ball came loose) prevented the Hogs from taking what would have been an insurmountable 10–0 lead. Given new life, Texas marched the length of the field for a late touchdown that gave the Longhorns a 7–3 victory. Had Brabham scored, the Hogs would have finished the regular season 10–0 and met LSU in the Cotton Bowl rather than facing Ole Miss in the Sugar. Would a Cotton Bowl victory have lifted the Hogs into the No. 1 spot? Quite possibly.

After winning the national title in 1964, the Razorbacks had another chance in '65. The Hogs were 10–0 and ranked second nationally behind Michigan State. The Spartans lost to UCLA in the Rose Bowl but alas, the Razorbacks saw their 22-game winning streak snapped by LSU in the Cotton Bowl. Had Arkansas won that game, it would have been another national title.

In 1969 the Hogs had another shot. Arkansas and Texas were both 9–0 going into their regular-season finale, playing against each other. The Longhorns were ranked first, the Hogs second. Texas erased a 14–0 deficit with two fourth-quarter touchdowns and a two-point conversion to escape with a victory in what was dubbed the "Game of the Century." A win in the Cotton Bowl secured the national title for Texas. Had the game gone the other way, the Hogs would have been ranked No. 1 going into the Cotton Bowl.

Nevertheless, the 1960s were a fabulous decade for the Razorbacks. At a time when there were only four major bowls (Rose, Orange, Cotton, Sugar) and few others, Arkansas played on New Year's Day seven times in that 10-year span. The Hogs earned the host spot in the Cotton Bowl three times and played in four Sugar Bowls. The Razorbacks finished in the national top 10 seven times and won 82 games. Only Alabama (90) and Texas (86) won more during that period.

"We were very proud of what we were able to accomplish in the 1960s," said Broyles. "Every year, the Arkansas-Texas game was a national event. Every college football fan knew about the Razorbacks."

9 Wear Schoonover

The first Razorback to letter in four sports was Wear Schoonover, a spectacular athlete from Pocahontas, Arkansas.

In 1929 Wear Schoonover became the first All-American football player at Arkansas as well as in the Southwest Conference.

As a senior in football in 1929 he became the first Arkansas player to earn All-America honors *and* the first Southwest Conference player to be named first-team All-America. During the 1929 season he caught 33 passes for 342 yards and six touchdowns while playing end on offense. Those totals may not look like much today, but they were extraordinary during his era, when most teams didn't pass much. He once made an astronomical 13 receptions for 152 yards in a game against Baylor, which still stands as a Razorbacks single-game reception record. James Shibest (against SMU in 1984) and Jarius Wright (against Texas A&M in 2011) are the only Hogs to have tied Schoonover's record of 13 catches in a game.

Players went both ways during the 1920s, and Schoonover was just as good on defense as he was on offense. In fact, he made five interceptions in one game against Texas A&M. (No other Razorback has made more than three interceptions in a game, and that has happened only five times.) He also had a 96-yard interception return for a touchdown against Centenary.

During his sophomore and junior years, Schoonover's coach for football and basketball was Francis Schmidt. His football career benefitted when Fred Thomsen, a passing coach ahead, replaced Schmidt, who moved to TCU.

Arkansas didn't have a basketball team until the 1923–24 season, but Schoonover helped the Hogs get to the top in a hurry. The Razorbacks won Southwest Conference championships in each of his three varsity seasons with a combined record of 33–3 in SWC games, including his senior season under head coach Charles Bassett. The Hogs were undefeated during his sophomore year, and their combined record in his three seasons was 54–9. And since there was no NCAA Tournament at the time, when Schoonover's basketball regular season ended, he went straight to baseball and track.

After graduating in 1930 with a 3.85 grade point average, Schoonover helped the football team as an assistant coach while attending law school. He earned his law degree in 1935.

Schoonover served in the navy for three and a half years during World War II, then spent the rest of his career in the Legal Services Department of the United States Department of Agriculture.

In 1967 he was elected to the National College Football Hall of Fame. He also is in the Arkansas Sports Hall of Fame as well as the University of Arkansas Sports Hall of Honor.

1978 Orange Bowl

Arkansas' 1977 football season, its first under the direction of head coach Lou Holtz, was a well-kept secret until near the end of the campaign. Frank Broyles had retired after the '76 campaign, and little was expected in Holtz's first year. Yet the Razorbacks' lone setback was a 13–9 defeat to Texas. With two games left to play in the season, Arkansas was hosting SMU in Fayetteville, and while most national media had pegged Penn State to play in the Orange Bowl, Holtz knew the Hogs were in good shape for a trip to Miami.

These were the days before the bowls were locked into any arrangements for any teams other than conference champions. The Southwest Conference winner, in this season Texas, went to the Cotton Bowl. Other league members were up for grabs. As Arkansas put the finishing touches on its victory over SMU, Hogs fans pelted the field with oranges. "Thank goodness we aren't going to the Gator Bowl," Holtz quipped.

Ranked sixth nationally with a 10–1 record, Arkansas was paired against second-ranked Oklahoma, the Big 8 champion and another of Barry Switzer's juggernauts. The Sooners were a mild favorite until Holtz was forced to make a jolting decision. Because of a major violation of team rules, Holtz suspended running backs Ben Cowins and Michael Forrest and wide receiver Donny Bobo. The three accounted for 78 percent of Arkansas' regular-season touchdowns. After Holtz's shocking announcement, the game was taken off the board and no one outside of Arkansas' dressing room and the 17,000 Razorback fans who made the trip to Miami expected the Hogs to win.

Somehow, though, Holtz remained confident. Broyles, then the athletic director, recalled the scene. "Lou came into my office before the team left for Miami and asked me if he thought we would win the national championship if we beat Oklahoma by three touchdowns."

Holtz had spotted a hole in the Oklahoma defense and knew it could be exploited. Backup running back Roland Sales would have a chance to be a hero, and quarterback Ron Calcagni would be called upon to execute the plan. Even though few teams in that era had been able to slow the Sooners' wishbone attack, Arkansas had a rock-solid defense spearheaded by tackles Dan Hampton and Jimmy Walker, and linebackers Larry Jackson and William Hampton fronted a stellar secondary.

All the major bowls were played on the same day then. That year, the Rose Bowl went long, delaying the start of the Orange Bowl. Holtz told jokes in the locker room to keep his team loose as the Hogs waited to take the field for kickoff. When asked why his team looked so fired up coming out of the tunnel, Holtz joked, "I told them the last 11 out had to start the game."

The rest of the jokes were all on OU. The Sooners fumbled on the game's third play and the Hogs recovered on the Oklahoma 9-yard line. Calcagni picked up eight yards on first down and Sales scored on second. After another OU fumble, this time at the Hogs 42, Calcagni directed a 58-yard drive and scored from the 1. Arkansas held a 14–0 lead going into halftime.

"We were feeling good in the dressing room," Calcagni recalled. "We knew how explosive Oklahoma was but we thought we could stop them. We also knew we were moving the ball on them."

Steve Little kicked a field goal on the first series of the third quarter and Sales bolted into the end zone from four yards out to cap 82-yard drive and make it 24–0. Texas had lost earlier in the day to Notre Dame, so an OU victory would have given the Sooners the national championship, but Oklahoma didn't deliver. The Hogs ultimately finished with a 31–6 win.

"Coach Holtz had a brilliant game plan," Calcagni said. "We knew their weaknesses and they never slowed us down. Our defense was great. They recovered three OU fumbles and made big plays all night."

The next day Holtz lobbied for the national championship, but Notre Dame leapfrogged from No. 5 to No. 1 on the strength of its win over Texas. Arkansas finished No. 3 in the national polls, and Holtz became an instant legend.

11 Original Southwest Conference Member

In the early days of college football there were no true conference alliances. A few sprang up, then disappeared. Arkansas played mostly southern schools in the early days and even earned the title "football champion of the South" with an undefeated season in 1909.

In 1913, the athletic director at the University of Texas invited eight schools—Arkansas, Texas, Texas A&M, Oklahoma, Baylor, Oklahoma A&M (later Oklahoma State), Southwestern (Texas), and Louisiana State—to a meeting with the idea of forming a conference. All eight said yes, and the Southwest Intercollegiate Athletic Conference became reality. In 1914, the schools met again and Arkansas, Texas, Texas A&M, Oklahoma, Oklahoma A&M, Baylor, and Southwestern became charter members; LSU decided not to join. Rice said yes but left the league two years later.

However, just because there was a league didn't mean the teams played each other. In 1915, Arkansas met only Oklahoma and Oklahoma A&M. Gradually the league began to take shape. SMU

Early Arkansas football games were played on the east side of campus.

joined in 1918; Southwestern dropped out the same year. Rice rejoined, but Oklahoma left in 1919. Oklahoma A&M said good-bye after the 1924 season. Phillips University (Oklahoma) joined in 1920 but left after a year. By 1925 it was Texas, Texas A&M, Rice, TCU, SMU, Baylor, and Arkansas—and that's the way it remained until Texas Tech joined in 1956 and the University of Houston became a member in 1976.

It was the late 1930s when the league instituted a round-robin schedule. The Texas schools were strong in football. There was a time the Texas schools considered asking Arkansas to leave, but Arkansas survived. The Razorbacks hung around long enough to emerge as decent in the 1950s and a national power in the 1960s.

During the 1970s and '80s, the SWC was as strong as any conference in the country. Arkansas, Texas, Houston, SMU, and Texas A&M each spent time in the nation's top 10. "People tend to forget that at one time the SWC was every bit as competitive as the SEC is today," said Harold Horton, former UA player, assistant coach, and president of the Razorback Foundation. "We played in the Orange Bowl, the Sugar Bowl, and the Fiesta Bowl, but never made it to the

Cotton Bowl during my years because the league was so strong," said Lou Holtz, Arkansas head football coach from 1977–83.

Frank Broyles, who coached the Razorbacks during their greatest decade (the 1960s, when the Hogs and Texas dominated the league) could see a changing landscape in the late 1980s. Arkansas was the only non-Texas school in the conference, and Broyles didn't think that boded well for future TV contracts or attendance.

On August 1, 1990, Arkansas announced it was leaving the SWC to join the Southeastern Conference. With UA's departure, it was the beginning of the end for the storied league. The SWC never added another member; it played its final football season in 1995. Texas, Texas A&M, Texas Tech, and Baylor paired with members of the Big 8 to form the Big 12. A&M has since left that league to become an SEC member, leaving room for TCU to rejoin its former Texas brethren in the Big 12. Houston, Rice, and SMU have bounced around other leagues.

It's hard to imagine now, but for decades the SWC competed with the best. Now it belongs only to history.

12 Moving to the Southeastern Conference

Always a visionary in college athletics, Frank Broyles feared for the future of the Southwest Conference in the late 1980s. The conference was comprised of Arkansas and eight schools from Texas. Broyles figured that if the college landscape changed, Arkansas could be left behind unless it made a bold move.

"Arkansas, Texas, and Texas A&M were strong, but SMU had been rocked by scandal. And TCU, Rice and Houston had trouble filling half of their stadiums," Broyles said. "Competition from the pros hurt TCU, SMU, Rice, and Houston considerably."

Broyles thought the Southeastern Conference would be a perfect fit for the Razorbacks. He and Tennessee athletic director Doug Dickey had been friends since Dickey was an assistant football coach on Broyles' staff at Arkansas. He asked Dickey to arrange a meeting on his behalf with SEC commissioner Harvey Schiller.

"The three of us played golf together so we wouldn't arouse any suspicion," Broyles said. "We didn't want any media to think there was anything to our meeting other than a friendly round of golf."

However, during the round Broyles told Schiller that if the SEC considered expansion at any time, Arkansas was interested. At

Welcome to the SEC

Arkansas had won three straight Southwest Conference basketball championships just before leaving for the Southeastern Conference. The Razorbacks were SWC champs in 1989, 1990, and 1991. They also won eight NCAA Tournament games during that time, reaching the Final Four in 1990 and the Elite Eight a year later. When the Hogs entered the SEC the conference landscape could best be described as Kentucky and everyone else. No SEC member other than the Wildcats had won a basketball national championship.

Todd Day, Lee Mayberry, and Oliver Miller were seniors on the 1992 team that made Arkansas' first-ever visit to Kentucky's Rupp Arena. Rick Pitino was the Kentucky coach—and he was waiting for UA coach Nolan Richardson. Since Richardson was well known for wearing stylish cowboy boots, Pitino, who dressed as if ready for the cover of *GQ*, came out in cowboy boots as well. He pointed them out to Richardson before the game and Nolan laughed accordingly. But when the Razorbacks led at halftime it was no longer a laughing matter. Pitino discarded the boots and returned to his normal high-style look in the second half. The wardrobe change didn't help. With Miller grabbing rebounds and making length of the court passes to Mayberry, Day, and others, the Hogs stunned the Wildcats 105–88. Arkansas went on to win the SEC regular season championship. It was a fitting welcome to the SEC.

the time the Hogs were winning championships in just about every men's sport in the SWC.

Nothing happened during Schiller's time, but when Roy Kramer became SEC commissioner in 1990, Broyles made sure he knew of Arkansas' interest in joining. The secret was well kept. Only as late as a day or two before Broyles called a press conference for August 1, 1990, was there any suspicion such a move was in the works.

"It was a very bold move on Coach Broyles' part," said Jeff Long, who replaced Broyles as athletic director after Broyles retired. "It was the first step in changing the landscape of college athletics."

Broyles noted, "The Southwest Conference wasn't going to last. The SEC was our best opportunity. It was a good fit geographically and we already had a good rivalry with Ole Miss. I knew our fans would enjoy games with Alabama, LSU, and the others."

However, with football schedules set long in advance, Arkansas had to play two more football seasons in the SWC before all sports could compete in the SEC. During the 1991–92 academic year, every other Arkansas team had an SEC schedule except the football team, which had to play against a group of Texas schools that were angry about Arkansas' secession.

"In the SEC they slit your throat and drink your blood," said defensive coordinator Joe Kines after he learned of the move. Kines had previously been an assistant at several SEC schools. In 1992, Arkansas' initial football season in the conference, he served as interim head coach after Jack Crowe was fired following a season opening loss to the Citadel.

Joining the SEC spurred a facilities update at Arkansas that would allow the Razorbacks to be competitive on all fronts. First came plans for the construction of Bud Walton Arena for basketball. Later it was Baum Stadium for baseball and Bogle Park for softball. The Randal Tyson Track Center was built and became the finest indoor track and field facility in the country. Later John McDonnell Field insured that Arkansas would have the finest outdoor facilities in track and field, too. Tennis, soccer, and golf teams received new digs as well.

The move to the SEC has been a major boon for University of Arkansas athletics. And it all started on a golf course on which three men plotted a future that would change the shape of college athletics.

13 The Big Shootout

During the late 1960s and most of the 1970s, long before ESPN was even a glimmer in Bill Rasmussen's eye, ABC was king of the college football television world. So to be selected for a national telecast was a big, big deal. Roone Arledge, head of ABC Sports, was looking for a blockbuster finale for the 1969 season, officially the 100th year in college football.

Arledge and his staff studied the collegiate landscape and noted that Arkansas was 10–1. The Hogs had beaten Georgia in the Sugar Bowl in 1968. Texas, meanwhile, won the Southwest Conference, and beat Tennessee in the Cotton Bowl. Both Arkansas and UT had most of their starters returning in 1969. The two teams were already staples for TV, so ABC asked the schools to reschedule their October showdown to December 6. Frank Broyles of Arkansas and Darrell Royal of Texas agreed and the game was on. It would be the last regular-season game of the decade and the only game played that day. Though they had high hopes for an exciting matchup, even ABC could not have envisioned the scenario that would develop.

Jim Bell was the new sports information director at Arkansas and he figured the December 6 date would give the Razorbacks a

President Richard Nixon was among the attendees at the 1969 "Big Shootout" between Arkansas and Texas.

wonderful opportunity to attract sportswriters from all over the country since they wouldn't be covering other games. So he invited reporters from every major newspaper, even though the UA press box only had about 50 available seats.

Arkansas and Texas rolled through their schedules and were both 9–0. Texas was ranked second nationally and Arkansas was third. Meanwhile, Ohio State was also 9–0 and ranked No. 1 before its annual battle with Michigan. *Sports Illustrated* tagged the Buckeyes as the "best team in college football history," but somehow Ohio State stumbled against the Wolverines. Suddenly Texas and Arkansas were ranked No. 1 and 2 going into the game at Fayetteville.

Bell was overwhelmed. Nearly every important sportswriter, even Jim Murray from the *Los Angeles Times*, had accepted his invitation. George Billingsley, an ardent Razorbacks fan, found housing for most of the national media at Bella Vista Village. The press box was far from adequate, but many of the writers happily watched the game from the sidelines. Billy Graham gave the invocation and President of the United States Richard Nixon was in attendance. The president and his Secret Service entourage were treated to prime seats by Razorbacks fans who were willing to give them up.

The game lived up to its billing. Arkansas led 14–0 after three quarters, and had lost another touchdown to a penalty. Then Texas scored twice in the final period and made a successful two-point conversion after its first score to steal a 15–14 victory.

It was the most disappointing setback in Razorbacks history. Broyles never watched the film. Texas advanced to the Cotton Bowl and beat Notre Dame to win the national championship. Arkansas went to the Sugar Bowl, but the team hadn't recovered emotionally. They lost to Ole Miss and quarterback Archie Manning.

Despite the disappointment of defeat, those who experienced that December day in Fayetteville will never forget it. It was labeled the "Game of the Century" in the Southwest Conference and still carries that title decades later.

14 Powder River Play

There was nothing special about Arkansas football going into the 1954 season. In fact, the Hogs were having a horrible decade. They had won only 12 games in the previous four seasons. In the previous year, they posted a dismal 3–7 record. Meanwhile, Ole Miss was a national powerhouse. The Rebels were unbeaten, ranked fifth nationally, and had outscored their opponents 171–35 in their first five games in 1954. Then they invaded Little Rock to play the Razorbacks.

Stunningly, the Hogs were unbeaten in 1954 as well. Bowden Wyatt, the second-year coach, had turned his lean group of players into the "25 Little Pigs," and they surprised everyone early on. They even won at Texas for the first time in 17 years.

A sellout crowd, one of the first ever at War Memorial Stadium, watched a scoreless game for three quarters. Then, with just a little more than six minutes left in the game, Wyatt sent in the second team backfield and called for the "Powder River Play." It was a play he ran as head coach at Wyoming and was named after a river in that state.

Buddy Bob Benson took the snap and ran to his left. So did the entire Ole Miss defense. Benson suddenly stopped and threw back to his right to Preston Carpenter, the blocking back, who rarely was involved in the passing game other than receiving the occasional swing pass out of the backfield.

Carpenter had his cover man beat, caught the ball at the Ole Miss 33, and sprinted the rest of the way to complete a 66-yard scoring play. Arkansas missed the extra point but it didn't matter; the Razorbacks won 6–0. Afterward, fans wouldn't leave the stadium. It was the Hogs' biggest win at Little Rock to that point in history and remains one of the most significant victories in UA history.

"I had 4.7 speed in the 40 but everyone always told me I was too slow," said Carpenter. "But Billy Kinard was covering me and I was behind him. As I watched the ball coming, my only thought was to catch it. I knew what Coach Wyatt would do to me if I didn't catch it."

Benson and Carpenter became instant legends. Carpenter went on to a long career as a receiver in the National Football League.

"I'm glad so many people [remember] the play," Carpenter said, "but I didn't think it was anything special. People came out of the stands after the game and wanted to put me on their shoulders. Everyone was celebrating, but it was just another game to me."

Considering the victory served as a launching pad for building statewide interest in the Razorbacks, it was more than just another game to Arkansas football.

15 Eddie Sutton

Arkansas' basketball program went from dominant in the 1920s and 1940s to practically dormant for more than two decades before Eddie Sutton was hired as head basketball coach in the spring of 1974. Promised renovations to Barnhill Fieldhouse (including an improved image in renaming it Barnhill Arena) and complete autonomy over the program, Sutton engineered a remarkable transition. In a few short years under Sutton's direction, basketball actually rivaled football in popularity among Razorbacks fans.

"I don't know if people know how hard it was for Eddie Sutton to get people in a football school in a football state to love basketball," said former ESPN college basketball analyst Jimmy Dykes, who also played for Sutton and now coaches Arkansas' women's basketball team. "The expansion of Barnhill Arena was a big deal, and when Sutton took the Triplets to the Final Four in 1978, Arkansas basketball was on the map."

The Triplets were Ron Brewer, Marvin Delph, and Sidney Moncrief, who first played together in Sutton's second year. In their final two seasons together, their Hogs teams were 58–6, won two Southwest Conference championships, beat second-ranked UCLA in the NCAA Tournament, and advanced to the Final Four.

"Coach Sutton kept telling us how good we were," Brewer said. "My junior year we were 26–2 but lost in the first round of the NCAA Tournament. We thought that set us up for the following year, but Coach Sutton told us we really didn't know how good we were that year. We get a lot of credit for our success, but we had great coaches. Coach Sutton gave us great game plans and schemes. We benefitted."

Sutton did it with discipline and defense. His teams played tenacious man-to-man defense and were disciplined enough on offense to work for a high-percentage shot. He was fortunate to have Brewer, Moncrief, and Delph, all three 6'4", highly athletic Arkansas natives, come along at the same time.

However, the hallmark of Sutton's teams were its premier guards. And indeed, Darrell Walker and Alvin Robertson were just as smothering on defense as Brewer and Moncrief were. Sutton also believed in having a solid big man to score inside, and he recruited some of the best in school history, including Scott Hastings, Joe Kleine, and Steve Schall.

Sutton's biggest accomplishment, as noted by Dykes, was putting Arkansas basketball on the map. He coached the Razorbacks for 11 seasons, and his last nine teams advanced to the NCAA Tournament at a time when there were fewer teams in the field. His teams won five Southwest Conference championships and finished second five times.

"Coach Sutton was good with X's and O's, putting personnel together, and creating a structure that was successful," said Brewer. "He was an incredible coach. He taught me a lot that helped me in the pros. I didn't always agree with him, but years later I told him I felt so close to him that it was like having a second dad. I'm not sure I realized how important to me he was until much later."

Sutton used the bond he had with his players to the maximum effect. In 1978, the Razorbacks climbed to number one in the

Associated Press poll, the first time they ever had accomplished the feat. The Hogs even made the cover of *Sports Illustrated* that year. It was an amazing time for a program that had never before received national attention.

The victories became intoxicating. The Hogs beat top-ranked North Carolina—featuring Michael Jordan—in 1984 at Pine Bluff. And their NCAA Tournament victory over UCLA came when the Bruins weren't far removed from the glory of the John Wooden era. Additionally, Arkansas beat Houston when the Cougars were ranked No. 2 and featured "Phi Slamma Jamma."

Barnhill Arena became an intimidating place to play, and even enlarged to 9,000 from 5,000, it couldn't accommodate all the Razorbacks fans who craved season tickets.

Sutton built a record of 260–75 before leaving to become head coach at Kentucky. His winning percentage of .776 is second only to Francis Schmidt, the program's first coach, who won 83.7 percent of his games from 1924 to 1929.

16 Darren McFadden

As freshman Darren McFadden split two speedy Georgia defenders and raced to a long touchdown run, legendary Bulldogs radio announcer Larry Munson exclaimed, "That's what everyone has been talking about! We [Georgia] need someone like that!"

During the three years McFadden was at Arkansas, no other team had anyone like him. In fact, the closest competitor may have been his own teammate, Felix Jones. Twice McFadden won the Doak Walker Award as the best running back in the country, and he was the runner-up in the Heisman Trophy voting two years in

Running back Darren McFadden shows off his rushing prowess in a 2007 game against Auburn. (AP Images)

a row. He was a two-time consensus All-American and three times a consensus All-Southeastern Conference.

"Darren took your breath away," said Houston Nutt, McFadden's head coach at Arkansas. "The first time he touched the ball it was obvious he was electrifying. He ran at a different speed. He had the heart of a lion as a competitor. And he loved to practice. It's a cliché for a coach to say a player was the first one to arrive at practice and the last to leave, but that was always the case with Darren. We had to tell him he had to leave and go get dinner."

By the time McFadden left Arkansas he had totally rewritten the school record book in rushing. He smashed Ben Cowins' 30-year-old record for career rushing yards, finishing with 4,590 yards—more than 1,000 more than Cowins. His single-season totals of 1,830 yards as a junior and 1,647 as a sophomore are the top two in school history. Third place trails by nearly 300 yards. McFadden also remains the only Razorback ever to rush for more than 1,000 yards three times during his career, combining his 1,113 yards as a freshman with his two record-breaking totals.

During the 2007 season, his last at Arkansas, McFadden earned more than 100 yards rushing in a school-record 10 games with a single-game best of 321 yards in a victory over South Carolina. His effort against the Gamecocks also tied the SEC's single-game record. He is the only Razorback to ever rush for 200 or more yards in a single game three separate times.

He also finished with a bang. In his last regular-season game he ran for 206 yards and scored three touchdowns as Arkansas upset top-ranked LSU in triple overtime.

He could block, too. Nutt recalled, "On Sundays, Darren and Felix Jones would be in the front row of the film room because they loved watching special teams video. Darren would tell everyone to watch the blocks he threw for Felix on kickoff returns."

McFadden bypassed his senior year to enter the NFL Draft and was a first-round pick (fourth overall) of the Oakland Raiders. Even though he played just three seasons at Arkansas, his rushing totals may never be approached by any future Razorback.

17 Felix Jones

If Felix Jones had not come along at the same time as Darren McFadden, he might be remembered as the best running back in Razorbacks history. He ran for 2,956 yards in three seasons, a remarkable accomplishment when considering McFadden earned another 4,590 during the same period. How many more yards would Jones have gained had he not shared time with McFadden?

McFadden had 785 career carries; Jones had 386. McFadden averaged 5.85 yards per attempt, a terrific number considering his total attempts. Jones averaged a school-record 7.66 yards per carry, and set the single-season record with an average of 8.74 yards per attempt in 2007.

Both rushers also returned kickoffs, but Jones was superior in that department. McFadden averaged 24.4 yards on 38 kickoff returns, but Jones set the UA standard with a 28.2-yard average on 62 returns. In addition, he scored three touchdowns.

"Felix was very fluid, fast, had great moves, and had eyes for returning kickoffs," said his coach, Houston Nutt. "He had the perfect timing of letting his blockers set up. McFadden was one of our best blockers when Felix returned kicks. They were great friends, never jealous of each other, and were such great teammates."

Jones still has the top two single-season yards-per-return averages in UA history. He returned 17 kicks for an average of 31.9 yards in 2005, then ran back 22 kicks in 2007 for an average of 29.6 yards. Jones entered the NFL Draft at the same time as his battery mate and was a first-round pick himself, selected by the Dallas Cowboys, 22nd overall.

Ken Hatfield

One of the finest defensive backs and punt returners in Razorbacks history, Ken Hatfield returned to Arkansas as head football coach in December 1983. In six years, he built the best winning percentage (.760) in school history. Three of his teams won 10 games in a season at a time when schools played 11 regular-season contests and there were no league championship games. His final two teams won Southwest Conference titles.

"Growing up in Texarkana, then West Helena, we were all Razorback fans," Hatfield said. "The principal at West Helena gave me a T-shirt with a huge Razorback on it. I wore it every day for a month. Finally, everyone asked my mom to take it off me and wash it.

"My brother, Dick, was a year ahead of me and was offered a partial scholarship so he went to Fayetteville. Coach [Wilson] Matthews recruited me because he knew my mother well.

"Our freshman team went 5–0, then I played as a sophomore, junior, and senior. The only regular-season game we lost in 1962, my sophomore year, was to Texas, when they scored with 37 seconds left. We had that game won but fumbled at the goal line when we would have gone ahead 10–0."

Hatfield then led the nation in punt returns in 1963 and '64 and had the famous 81-yard return in Arkansas' critical 1964 victory at Texas. That was the victory that gave the Hogs the confidence to win them all and earn the post-bowl consensus for the national title.

"We had a stigma about beating Texas back then," Hatfield said. "Once we beat them, Arkansas knew it could beat Texas. We beat

John McDonnell

Yes, this is a book dedicated to Razorbacks football and basketball. But no Razorbacks fan should die without knowing about John McDonnell, the winningest coach in the history of college athletics. A recent biography, *John McDonnell* by Andrew Maloney and John McDonnell, details his extraordinary life. This space is too short to acknowledge all of his accomplishments, but consider this: a native of County Mayo, Ireland; cross country All-American at Southwestern Louisiana; and one-time cameraman for *The Soupy Sales Show* as well New York Mets baseball games, McDonnell coached the Razorback track program to 42 national championships. That's not a misprint. The number is right: *42*. And his teams won 84 conference championships. That's right, 84 (38 in the Southwest Conference and 46 in the Southeastern Conference). He coached 185 All-Americans. His teams won 34 straight conference cross country championships, half in the SWC and the other half in the SEC. Quite simply, there will never be another coach like him.

them when they were at their best. They had a 19-game winning streak at the time and were defending national champions."

Hatfield hadn't planned on going into coaching, but while in the military he was asked to be an assistant coach at West Point. That led to assistant coaching jobs at Tennessee, Florida, and the Air Force Academy before he was named head coach at Air Force.

Back-to-back victories against Notre Dame brought him national recognition, and after the 1983 season he was lured back to his alma mater as head coach.

"I came on faith it was the right place God wanted us," said Hatfield. "I never talked contract, including how many years and how much I was getting paid. It didn't worry me. I did it for the love of Arkansas."

Hatfield's love for Arkansas was contagious. His first team finished 7–4–1 and was in every game until the finish. Only a narrow season-ending loss to SMU kept the Hogs out of the Cotton Bowl. His next two squads played in the Holiday and Orange Bowl games, and his final two were SWC champions and played in the Cotton Bowl.

Unfortunately, Hatfield's relationship with Broyles turned tense, and Hatfield left Arkansas following the 1989 season to become head coach at Clemson. He later was head coach at Rice.

When his coaching career ended, he moved back to northwest Arkansas, where he remains a beloved member of the community.

19 22 in a Row

After four sensational years that featured three Southwest Conference championships; 34 victories in 44 games; and trips to the Gator, Cotton, and Sugar (twice) Bowls, Arkansas was tapped to win the SWC title in 1963. Instead, the Razorbacks lost close games to Baylor and eventual national champion Texas in their second and third conference games, and never recovered.

After a 14–7 loss at SMU the Hogs were 4–5, despite not losing a game by more than seven points. On the plane ride home, several of the underclassmen approached head coach Frank Broyles about preparing for 1964 right away.

"We were finishing the season the next week against Texas Tech at Fayetteville," recalled Jim Lindsey, a sophomore on the '63 squad. "We asked Coach Broyles to treat the week like it was spring practice, with full-scale scrimmaging. We wanted to make sure we were more prepared in 1964."

Broyles admitted he had been easier on his players in 1963 because he appreciated the success the Hogs had produced in the previous seasons. "A coach tends to be a little softer when players have performed so well," Broyles said. "You want to reward them. But that can backfire. You aren't as good at the little things that make a difference between winning and losing. We lost five very close games in 1963. We didn't have a great year but we learned a lot and didn't make the same mistake the following year."

So the Razorbacks scrimmaged throughout that last week in 1963 and were more than ready for Texas Tech. Then the game almost didn't happen. The day before the Hogs were set to host the Red Raiders, the President of the United States, John F. Kennedy, was shot and killed in Dallas.

Texas Tech's football team was already on the way by plane, so Arkansas decided to play the game as scheduled. Some colleges played their matchups, others canceled in the wake of the assassination. NFL games were also played that Sunday, a controversial decision which is chronicled in the Dan Rather–narrated documentary *Rozelle's Decision to Play*. In Fayetteville, it may not have been as festive an atmosphere as normal, but the game was crucial. The Razorbacks defeated the Red Raiders 27-20 to start what would become its school-record winning streak.

All the off-season work between the victory over Texas Tech and the 1964 season opener paid off. The Hogs were lean, mean, and exceptionally quick as they started the '64 campaign. In fact, they didn't have a defensive lineman that weighed as much as 200 pounds. Nose guard Jimmy Johnson, the heaviest, weighed in at 195. Nonetheless the Razorbacks were stout on defense. A midseason victory over defending national champion and No. 1-ranked Texas vaulted the Hogs to a 10–0 record.

"When we were getting ready to play Nebraska in the Cotton Bowl after the regular season, I told the sportswriters that we didn't have a player on defense that weighed 200 pounds," recalled Broyles. "They didn't believe me, so I invited them to our dressing room before one of our practices. I had our defensive starters step

Breaking Down the Streak

Through the years, much has been written and said about the greatest winning streak in Razorbacks football history. Beginning with an important victory against Texas Tech to close the 1963 season, the streak continued until being ended at the hands of LSU in the 1966 Cotton Bowl.

Here's a game-by-game look at the results:

November 23, 1963:	Arkansas vs. Texas Tech	27–20
September 19, 1964:	Arkansas vs. Oklahoma State	14–10
September 26, 1964:	Arkansas vs. Tulsa	31–22
October 3, 1964:	Arkansas at TCU	29–6
October 10, 1964:	Arkansas vs. Baylor	17–6
October 17, 1964	Arkansas at Texas	14–13
October 24, 1964	Arkansas vs. Wichita State	17–0
October 31, 1964	Arkansas at Texas A&M	17–0
November 7, 1964	Arkansas vs. Rice	21–0
November 14, 1964	Arkansas vs. SMU	44–0
November 21, 1964	Arkansas at Texas Tech	17–0
November 28, 1964	Arkansas vs. Nebraska*	10–7
September 18, 1965	Arkansas vs. Oklahoma State	28–14
September 25, 1965	Arkansas vs. Tulsa	20–12
October 2, 1965	Arkansas vs. TCU	28–0
October 9, 1965	Arkansas at Baylor	38–7
October 16, 1965	Arkansas vs. Texas	27–24
October 23, 1965	Arkansas vs. North Texas State	55–20
October 30, 1965	Arkansas vs. Texas A&M	31–0
November 6, 1965	Arkansas at Rice	31–0
November 13, 1965	Arkansas at SMU	24–3
November 20, 1965	Arkansas vs. Texas Tech	42–24

Cotton Bowl, Dallas, TX

on the scales and, sure enough, none of them were as heavy as 200 pounds. Nebraska's fullback, Harry Wilson, weighed 235. He was bigger than any of our defenders."

A late Bobby Burnett touchdown gave Arkansas a Cotton Bowl victory over Nebraska. The post-bowl versions of the national championship served as reward for just the second (1909 was the other) unbeaten season in school history.

Bill Gray was the quarterback for the first two games of the 1964 season, then Fred Marshall returned from an injury to direct the final nine victories. Both passers were gone in 1965, but the replacement was more than up to the task. A junior who had red-shirted in '64 and ultimately would have a song written about him, Jon Brittenum was indeed a "Quarterbackin' Man." He led the Hogs to another unbeaten regular season.

Only the Texas game was a struggle. The Hogs led 20–0, gave up 24 straight to trail, then won 27–24 on a late one-yard quarter-back sneak for a touchdown by Brittenum. While the 1964 team had relied on a defense that shut out its last five regular season foes, the '65 Razorbacks had a prolific offense that produced 324 points in 10 games—a very high total for that era.

Heavily favored in the Cotton Bowl against LSU, the Razorbacks had a difficult time stopping the Tigers' running game. Worse, Brittenum suffered a shoulder separation in the first half. He played in the second half despite the injury but the Hogs offense was not the same. LSU snapped Arkansas' 22-game winning streak when it won the game 14-7.

"It was a hard way for the winning streak to end," Broyles said. "Most Arkansas fans think of the 1969 loss to Texas as the most disappointing defeat we ever suffered, and there is no doubt that was painful. But losing to LSU in the Cotton Bowl was just as disappointing. We would have won back-to-back national champi-onships—and very few schools ever have that opportunity."

Still, 22 in a row is quite a streak. It remains the longest in school history.

Seven Overtimes

Do you know when Arkansas played its last tied football game? It happened in 1993, when the Hogs missed an extra point after an early touchdown and ended up tying Mississippi State 13–13 in Little Rock. Shortly thereafter the NCAA instituted overtime rules to prevent games from ending in ties.

Arkansas' first-ever overtime prevented another 13–13 tie with Mississippi State. The Hogs kicked a field goal in the extra period to win 16–13 at Starkville in 1996. The Hogs beat Mississippi State in overtime again in 2000. But it was the third time that was really the charm for Arkansas: the Hogs set the bar for longest college football game in history in a record-breaking *seven*-overtime game.

After a 1–3 start, Arkansas had won three in a row when it arrived in Oxford to play Ole Miss in 2001. Zac Clark was the Razorbacks' starting quarterback, but freshman Matt Jones, playing sometimes at receiver, was emerging as a talented backup quarterback whose role was increasingly becoming more significant. Clark had started and played most of the game against the Rebels, but when regulation ended with the teams deadlocked at 17, Jones took over. (Actually, Jones had marched the Razorbacks to a fourth-quarter touchdown after not playing a down of quarterback in the first three periods, then remained for the extra action.)

"Ole Miss hadn't stopped our running game in the fourth quarter, so we kept it on the ground in overtime," Jones recalled. "They never did stop us."

Actually, the Rebels stopped the Hogs in overtime number two. Fortunately, Arkansas blanked Ole Miss in the second overtime, too. Thus, the game went on…and on…and on before finally being decided in the seventh overtime.

The Last Team with the Ball Wins

ESPN was in its infancy when it chose to televise the Arkansas-Baylor football game in 1981. Both teams boasted prolific offenses. Arkansas had defeated No. 1 Texas earlier in the year; Baylor was the defending Southwest Conference champion. At that time, ESPN could not show games live. Instead, they would show them tape-delayed a few hours later, then rerun the telecast throughout the week.

They couldn't have picked a better game for that format. The two teams combined for 80 points in a contest that wasn't decided until the final seconds. It was only the second start in the career of freshman quarterback Brad Taylor, who would eventually put up terrific passing numbers. That night, Arkansas' Jessie Clark was the star. He scored five touchdowns, a school record at the time. He ran behind one of the school's best-ever offensive lines, which featured Jay Bequette, Steve Korte, and Alfred Mohammed, among others.

The scoring went back and forth. Baylor led by 10; then Arkansas scored touchdowns on three straight possessions to grab an 11-point lead. Back came the Bears, who scored with less than two minutes to go to take a 39–38 lead. But they were stopped on a two-point conversion try. Trailing by one, Taylor took the Hogs down the field, with tight end Darryl Mason making a big catch to keep the drive alive. Mason had left the game earlier when his front teeth were knocked out by a jarring hit from Baylor safety Van McElroy. The Razorbacks moved close enough for Bruce Lahay, an All-American kicker that year, to try a field goal. Lahay kicked it through the uprights with seven seconds left and Arkansas had a 41–39 win. Indeed, whoever had the ball last would win. And on this night, it was Arkansas who had the advantage in Little Rock.

Jones scored touchdowns on runs of 25 and eight yards and had a 24-yard scoring pass to George Wilson, Mark Pierce had two scoring runs of two yards, and Cedric Cobbs had a 16-yard TD run for the Hogs. But Eli Manning and Ole Miss either answered or preceded the Razorbacks with touchdowns in each period.

Going into the seventh overtime, Jones was ready for it to end. He said, "I told John Thompson, our defensive coordinator, to stop them so we could go home." He held up his end of the bargain. After handing off to Pierce for a short touchdown blast, he hit DeCori Birmingham for the two-point conversion. Then the defense did its part. Ole Miss scored but Hogs linebacker Jermaine Petty stopped the two-point try short of the goal line. With that, the Razorbacks won a wild one, 58–56.

Jones overtime fireworks weren't through, though. After quarterbacking the Hogs through a six-overtime loss in 2002, he was at the helm at Kentucky when the Razorbacks and Wildcats finished regulation tied at 24.

Some of the same Razorbacks played prominent roles. Pierce scored twice, Wilson caught a touchdown pass, and Jones ran for one score and threw for two more. Yet the teams were still even after six overtimes.

In overtime number seven, DeCori Birmingham raced 25 yards for a touchdown on Arkansas' first play. Jones then passed to tight end Jason Peters for the two-point conversion. Kentucky was driving for the tying score when the Hogs caused and recovered a fumble that ended the game. Arkansas won 71–63.

"After the Ole Miss game, we were thrilled to win, but everyone was exhausted," Jones said. "I didn't even care about changing clothes. I just wanted to get on the plane and go home. I was just as tired after the Kentucky game. Those two nights are as tired as I've ever been."

Those two nights are as tired as *anyone* ever has been as they still stand as the longest games in college football history.

Ryan Mallett

Ryan Mallett grew up in Texarkana wanting to be a Razorback. As a 6'6" quarterback with a rocket arm, Mallett had his choice of schools—but he figured Arkansas wasn't one of them. After all, Mallett was in the same recruiting class as Springdale's Mitch Mustain, rated the No. 1 quarterback in the country. So when Mustain committed to Arkansas, Mallett began to look elsewhere.

"Elsewhere" turned out to be a long way from home. Mallett signed with Michigan and served as the backup quarterback as a true freshman. In fact, he even started three games when injury sidelined the Wolverines' starting quarterback. Things were going well for him in Ann Arbor, but he still wanted to go home. So when Mustain transferred from Arkansas to USC, Mallett knew his opportunity had come.

"I was ready to come back to the University of Arkansas," Mallett said. "I knew I would have to sit out a year. Houston Nutt was the coach when I made my decision but then he was gone. Bobby Petrino was the new coach, and I was fine playing for him.

"We were fortunate to have great receivers, and my first year we went 8–5 and won the Liberty Bowl. We thought we had a chance to have a great year in 2010 and we did. Even though our goal of winning the national championship didn't happen, we played in the Sugar Bowl. That was the first time Arkansas had ever played in a BCS bowl. We were very proud of that."

The Razorbacks earned a spot in the Sugar Bowl by beating LSU in the regular-season finale. Mallett—whose passes reached the receivers in less time than any Razorbacks quarterback since Joe Ferguson in the early 1970s—fired a strike to Cobi Hamilton for a

Native son Ryan Mallett fires a strike in the 2010 Liberty Bowl. (AP Images)

The Longest Throw

Brad Taylor had one of the strongest arms of any quarterback in Razorbacks history. He played three years for Lou Holtz and one for Ken Hatfield, passing for more than 4,800 career yards.

He grew up in the small town of Danville. Commenting on his small town's size, before Arkansas played in Texas A&M's 80,000-seat stadium one year, Taylor told ABC announcer Keith Jackson, "You could put a whole lot of Danvilles in here." A freshman in 1981, he became a starter when Tom Jones was hurt. He split time with Jones in 1982, then started alone in his last two years. Because he became a starter so early in his career, he bonded with the class that became seniors in 1982. "I even lived with Billy Ray Smith one summer," he said. The strongest Razorback in that class—and arguably in any class since—was Steve Korte, who once bench pressed 585 pounds. Korte heard Taylor could throw the ball 100 yards, and told Brad he wanted to see it for himself.

"I was a freshman and I figured if Steve Korte told you to do something, you did it," Taylor said. "I had never tried to throw the ball 100 yards before. I did it, but didn't think it was that big of a deal. When Coach Holtz found out, he chewed me out and told me not to risk hurting my arm by doing it again." As far as anyone knows, no Razorback ever has repeated the feat.

touchdown on the last play of the first half. Yet that's not the play Mallett remembered most.

"We had fourth-and-3 in LSU territory, and Coach Petrino made the decision to go for it. It was the fourth quarter. We were ahead by a point, so a field goal would have only made it a four-point lead. LSU had to think we would give it to Knile Davis or throw a short pass. Instead, Joe Adams made a great fake to draw the defender in and I threw it to him for a touchdown. That was the play I remember most [from] my entire career at Arkansas."

Another of his prime receivers, Jarius Wright, loved having Mallett in the huddle. "He was a great leader," Wright said. "He was outspoken in the huddle. Every pass he threw was hard; he only had one speed. But he still had great touch, especially on the deep pass. When he threw a deep pass he would put it right on your face mask."

Mallett only played two years before entering the NFL Draft. Picked by the New England Patriots, he spent the first three years of his career backing up, and understudying, Tom Brady. "Tom has been great to me," Mallett said. "But I want the opportunity to play. I know that opportunity will come at some point, maybe with another team."

In the meantime, Mallett has spent his off-seasons in Fayetteville because he so loves the area. "I want to own a ranch in the area to have someplace I can enjoy when football is over," he said.

When football was over for Mallett at Arkansas, he ranked as the school's career leading passer with 7,493 yards—even though he played only two years. However, his career record didn't stand long; Tyler Wilson broke it two years later. But Mallett still owns the single-season mark with 3,869 yards in 2010, and will forever be remembered as a standout passer on two great Hogs teams.

22 Lou Holtz

Midway through the 1976 season, Frank Broyles already had decided it would be his last as Arkansas head football coach. He told very few people. Since he was also athletic director, he began considering who would replace him. During his 19 years as Razorbacks coach, Broyles had employed many assistant coaches who went on to become successful head coaches. However, he didn't think the next coach had to be a former Razorback.

"I had met Lou Holtz at a coaches' golf tournament and liked him," Broyles recalled. "He and I stayed in contact because I knew he wanted to become a head coach at a major university."

Holtz's first head coaching job came at William & Mary. There he took the school to its first-ever bowl game. He then became head coach at North Carolina State, where his innovative offensive game plans transformed the Wolfpack into one of the most exciting teams in the Atlantic Coast Conference. After the 1975 season, Holtz accepted a head coaching position in the NFL with the New York Jets.

Unfortunately, it was not a good decision. Pro players are not into the *rah-rah* that inspires college players, nor do they like many rules. Holtz was miserable. He called Broyles to let him know he was interested in returning to college coaching. It was all Broyles needed to hear.

Broyles officially retired as coach after the last game of the 1976 season against Texas. Less than a week later, Holtz was announced as the new head coach.

Likely the smallest head coach (5'7" or so) in UA history, Holtz had a commanding presence. There was plenty of leftover talent from the Broyles era. The Hogs had been to the Cotton Bowl in 1975 but finished 5–5–1 in '76 after quarterback Ron Calcagni suffered a season-ending injury midway through the campaign.

The next season, Calcagni was back—and so was much of the defense. But, Arkansas was picked sixth in the nine-team Southwest Conference. The Razorbacks lost a midseason showdown with Texas, but that was it. Arkansas ran the rest of the table, finished 11–1, and defeated then-second-ranked Oklahoma 31-6 in the Orange Bowl. Just one year after a losing season, Arkansas finished ranked No. 3 in the nation.

"Coach Holtz knew how to bring out the best in you," Calcagni said. "Before the Orange Bowl, he had my confidence level extremely high. He put a lot of pressure on you in practice.

Almost the Bear

Since Paul "Bear" Bryant grew up in Fordyce, Arkansas, many often wondered why Arkansas never was able to hire him as head coach. It wasn't because of lack of effort. As early as 1941, a group of boosters thought Bryant was the ideal coach to replace Fred Thomsen. Bryant was an assistant at Vanderbilt at the time. But the attack on Pearl Harbor and beginning of World War II ended any potential pursuit, as Bryant enlisted in the navy.

After firing Otis Douglas at the end of the 1952 season, athletic director John Barnhill thought he had Bryant this time. The Bear was head coach at Kentucky, where he felt overshadowed by basketball coach Adolph Rupp. Bryant had led the Wildcats to three top 20 finishes and had defeated Oklahoma in the Sugar Bowl, but he wasn't sure anyone noticed. He was ready to come to Arkansas when a group of influential boosters convinced him to stay at Kentucky. He stayed only another year, again finishing in the top 20, then headed to Texas A&M.

Ultimately he went to Alabama, his alma mater, where he became a legend. Meanwhile, Barnhill turned to two coaches—Bowden Wyatt, who led the Razorbacks to the Cotton Bowl in his second year before leaving for Tennessee, and Jack Mitchell, who departed after three years to become head coach at Kansas—before hiring Frank Broyles, who would become a legend in his own right.

When he first came to Arkansas he told me I wasn't tough enough to play for him. He was motivating me. I hurt both of my thumbs in spring practice that first year and at one point had casts on both hands. But I played in the spring game to show him I was tough enough to play."

Holtz ultimately became a national celebrity. He appeared on *The Tonight Show with Johnny Carson* and performed magic tricks while making quips. He had dinner at the White House. Arkansas fans bought Lou Holtz dolls at the bookstores.

Sports Illustrated ranked Holtz's second team No. 1 in its preseason issue. A photographer spent a week with Holtz for the profile. There were tons of pictures of Holtz and the Razorbacks in that 1978 preseason magazine. The Razorbacks didn't end up winning the national title, but they earned nine victories and tied UCLA in the Fiesta Bowl.

The '79 Razorbacks featured a solid senior group and perhaps the best freshman class Holtz ever recruited. In fact, it was among the best classes in school history. Among them were Gary Anderson, Billy Ray Smith, Richard Richardson, Ron Matheny, Darryl Bowles, and several others who became starters in their first year. The Hogs were 10–1 in the regular season, but lost to national champion Alabama in the Sugar Bowl.

Holtz had dazzled the media at the Sugar Bowl press conferences, while Bear Bryant, nearing the end of his remarkable career, mostly mumbled. Holtz was devastated by the loss. "Coach Bryant told me it was the best game his team played all year," Holtz recalled. "I told him I was sure glad I got to see it."

Holtz's first three squads won 30 games. Even now, with more games on the schedule, no other Arkansas teams have accomplished that same feat.

The freshmen of '79 carried the Hogs for four years. Arkansas won 34 games during those four years and played in bowl games each season. They won the Hall of Fame and Bluebonnet Bowls and lost the Sugar and Gator Bowls.

There were still good players on campus but the talent level was thinned considerably after the 1979 group's eligibility expired. The Hogs slipped to 6–5 in 1983, and Holtz was asked to resign. His final tally in seven seasons was 60–21–2. Among his many accomplishments, Arkansas' win over Oklahoma in his first year is still regarded as one of the most significant victories in school history.

As any college football fan knows, Holtz's career didn't end at Arkansas. He coached two years at Minnesota before restoring the glory of the football program at Notre Dame, where he guided the Irish to a national championship and piloted the Fighting

Irish for more than a decade. He later coached at South Carolina, then became famous to a younger generation as studio cohost for ESPN's college football coverage.

The Triplets

The right place at the right time? That was Eddie Sutton when he became head basketball coach at the University of Arkansas. Why? Because three superior players from within Arkansas' borders were available to jump-start the program.

They were Marvin Delph of Conway, who was a freshman on Sutton's first team; Ron Brewer from Fort Smith, who transferred from Westark Junior College and played three years with the Razorbacks beginning with Sutton's second team; and Sidney Moncrief of Little Rock, who was a freshman during Sutton's second year. Collectively, they were known as "the Triplets," and they changed the face of Razorbacks basketball forever.

"The unique thing about us was we all knew each other from high school," said Brewer. "We had played against each other. When we were in high school I never thought in a million years we would play together at the University of Arkansas."

They not only played together, they put Razorbacks basketball on the map. In their three years as teammates, they led the Hogs to a staggering record of 77–15 (58–6 during their final two seasons). Arkansas had not been to the NCAA Tournament in 19 years before the 1976–77 campaign, when the Razorbacks finished 26–2, were 16–0 in the Southwest Conference, and won the SWC Tournament. They lost to Wake Forest in the first round of the NCAA tourney after Moncrief fouled out.

Arkansas won the SWC again the following year and defeated Weber State in a first-round NCAA Tournament game. The Razorbacks were matched with second-ranked UCLA in the second round. Al McGuire—who coached Marquette to the NCAA championship in 1977 then retired after a long career and became a color commentator for NBC—watched the Razorbacks edge UCLA as he prepared for his role in the regional finals telecast. He noticed that Delph, Brewer, and Moncrief were all the same height and extraordinarily athletic. While their talents were distinctively different, McGuire was the one who coined the nickname "the Triplets."

The moniker stuck, and the Hogs won the regional final to advance to the Final Four. Arkansas lost to Kentucky in the semifinals, then beat Notre Dame for third place on a last second shot by Brewer.

"We felt we should have been in the championship game," Brewer said. "We thought we were better than Kentucky and would have beaten them nine times if we had played 10 games. They were bigger than we were but we thought we were more talented. If we had it to do over, we would have pushed the ball and spread the floor more against them.

"Before the third place game I overheard Coach Sutton and [Notre Dame coach] Digger Phelps saying they shouldn't have to play a third-place game. Our players didn't feel that way. We weren't going to let Notre Dame beat us. We were tied with 10 seconds to go, and Coach Sutton called timeout. He told me to bring the ball up the court, penetrate, and look for Sidney.

"I knew I was going to take that shot, so there was no urgency to get into an offensive set. It was a solo job. I'm glad it went in."

Brewer's basket against Notre Dame was his last as a Razorback. Delph was gone, too, but Moncrief had another year of eligibility left. He led the Hogs to a 25–5 mark and a spot in the NCAA regional finals in 1979 before a season-ending two-point loss to top-ranked Indiana State, which was led by Larry Bird.

Retired Numbers

Arkansas had never retired a basketball jersey number until Sidney Moncrief came along. In fact, the school had a policy against retiring jersey numbers. Only No. 12 in football had been retired—and even that had been used once since being "retired." Clyde Scott wore No. 12 in the late 1940s; he consented to have the jersey used again in order for the Razorbacks to secure the recruiting signature of Steve Little, who became a two-time All-American placekicker. After Little finished in 1977, the number went back into the vault.

Razorbacks basketball coach Eddie Sutton, aware of the No. 12 precedent, pleaded with athletic director Frank Broyles to have Moncrief's No. 32 retired. Broyles relented. Moncrief's jersey hung in Barnhill Arena from 1980, the year after his graduation, until the Hogs moved to Bud Walton Arena. Somehow the enlarged jersey disappeared during the transition. But it was finally scheduled to be hung in Bud Walton in time for the 2014–15 season.

"Moncrief, Brewer, and Delph were exceptional talents," Sutton recalled. "They were winners. Those were great teams. The first year we went to the NCAA [Tournament], I'm not sure we realized how good we were. Sidney had the big valentine. His heart was as big as any player I coached. Brewer had quick hands and was a great scorer. Marvin was a terrific pure shooter."

Despite only playing three seasons, Brewer was Arkansas' third-leading scorer when his career ended. He always will be remembered for his last-second shot against Notre Dame, but he also had game-winning buzzer-beaters at Texas Tech and Baylor in his last two years.

Delph was the UA career leading scorer at the conclusion of his career. He didn't think much of it though. "Sidney will break the record next year," Delph predicted at the time. Indeed, Moncrief broke Delph's record. Moncrief still ranks second behind only Todd Day in career scoring with 2,066 points. He also had 1,015 rebounds, which stands the UA career record. The Razorbacks record during his four years was 102–20, including 6–3 in the NCAA Tournament and three SWC titles. For his part, Delph remains in the Razorbacks top 10 with 1,742 career points. What's perhaps more remarkable is that Delph had a career field goal percentage of .529, with easily more than half of his shots coming from what would now be three-point range.

"We were proud of what we accomplished, but even more important was the bond we formed," Brewer said. "We became best friends as well as teammates. It was the same with the other guys on the team, like Jim Counce and Steve Schall. We don't see each other as much anymore but to this day we are still best buddies."

Sutton truly was in the right place at the right time.

Billy Ray Smith Sr. and Jr.

Billy Ray Smith Sr. and his son, Billy Ray Smith Jr. each had distinguished careers as Arkansas Razorbacks and standouts in the National Football League.

Smith Sr., who grew up in Augusta, Arkansas, was a freshman for Bowden Wyatt's first team in 1953. His first varsity season was 1954, when the Razorbacks surprised everyone but themselves by winning the Southwest Conference championship. He was also a standout boxer while at the university. In 1956, he was named All-SWC as a defensive tackle.

Smith Sr. was picked by the Los Angeles Rams in the third round of the 1957 NFL Draft. He was the 26th player selected overall. (That would be a first-round pick today, but there were only 12 teams in the league at that time.) He spent just one year

*Billy Ray Smith Sr.
was All–Southwest
Conference at Arkansas
before becoming an
All-Pro defensive
lineman with Baltimore
in the NFL.*

in Los Angeles and three in Pittsburgh before becoming a star in Baltimore where he helped lead the Colts to two Super Bowls. He played in the Super Bowl game when the Colts lost to the New York Jets—and played his final game as a professional player in Baltimore's win over the Dallas Cowboys in Super Bowl V.

Smith Jr. never made it to the Super Bowl, but he played 10 years in the NFL with the San Diego Chargers after being the fifth player selected in the 1983 Draft. However, his collegiate career was much more glamorous than that of his father.

"I grew up around my dad and pro football," Smith said while with the Razorbacks. "I learned a lot from being around those players."

Lou Holtz, his coach at Arkansas, said Smith learned so much growing up that he "had a knack for knowing where the ball would be. He had great instincts. He deserved all the honors he received."

Smith Jr. was a two-time All-American and twice runner up for the Outland Trophy, given annually to the nation's best lineman.

He made 299 career tackles, including 63 behind the line of scrimmage—good for a whopping 343 yards in losses. His career numbers in tackles behind the line and yards in losses remain a school record; the mark hasn't been approached since he finished in 1982.

Both Smiths played on successful Arkansas teams. Billy Ray Sr. missed his junior season, but played on teams with a two-year record of 14–7. However, he played in only one bowl game, the 1955 Cotton Bowl.

Smith, Jr. started every game he played in, 48 in a row. The Razorbacks were 34–13–1 during that span and played in the Sugar, Hall of Fame, Gator, and Bluebonnet Bowl games.

Smith Sr. went on to a successful career in private business. He passed away in 2001. Junior turned to media work. He has served as color analyst for UCLA football, and currently hosts a daily radio show in San Diego.

The 25 Little Pigs

When Bowden Wyatt became Arkansas' head football coach prior to the 1953 football season, he knew major changes needed to be made. The '52 Razorbacks had gone 2–8 under Otis Douglas, even though there were several talented players on that team who later spent considerable time in the National Football League.

Douglas had been an assistant coach with the Philadelphia Eagles when he followed John Barnhill as head coach after the 1949 football season. He tailored his UA offense and defense after the Eagles, but lacked a staff that was skilled at teaching fundamentals to college athletes. Plus, Douglas' idea of treating his players like men was to give them the same liberty that professional players had. That meant little discipline.

Wyatt, on the other hand, was all about discipline. He also installed an extraordinarily physical approach. He wanted to make sure his team would be among the toughest in college football. His first spring practice was brutal. The ranks of players thinned considerably. The Hogs went 3–7 in his first year, but a solid foundation was being laid.

"Bear Bryant was famous for his preseason workouts at Junction when he was at Texas A&M," said Preston Carpenter, a sophomore on Wyatt's first team. "Their camp wasn't any harder than ours. In fact, I was at a banquet once with eight of the Junction Boys. I was struck by how small most of them were. I told them Junction wasn't anything compared to Bowden Wyatt's training camp. They all looked at me funny."

No one looked at the Hogs funny in 1954. There still weren't many of them on the squad. As a result, they became known as the "25 Little Pigs," because their numbers were still low. There may have been more than 25 on the team, but the nickname stuck.

The Razorbacks beat Tulsa 41–0, then earned their first victory in the state of Texas in six seasons with a 20–13 win over TCU. A narrow win over Baylor preceded Arkansas' first victory over Texas at Austin in 18 years. But it was their victory over fifth-ranked Ole Miss that gained them national respect.

Arkansas peaked at 7–0 and ranked fourth in the country before the lack of depth began to make a difference. SMU beat the Hogs by a touchdown, then LSU edged the Razorbacks by a point. A win over Houston in the season finale allowed Arkansas to finish 8-2. Prevailing as Southwest Conference champions, the Hogs hosted Georgia Tech in the Cotton Bowl.

Not even a one-touchdown loss to the Yellow Jackets could stem the wild enthusiasm Wyatt had created. His raw-boned squad won an unexpected league title. Fans raised $17,000 to buy Wyatt a new Cadillac. Then, just one week after the Cotton Bowl, Wyatt left the Razorbacks to become head coach at Tennessee, his alma mater. He was only at Arkansas for two years, but the 25 Little Pigs became one of the most legendary teams in school history.

26 Calling the Hogs

It is the most unique cheer in college athletics. The first time someone hears it, chills go up and down the spine. For longtime Razorbacks fans, the chills never stop, no matter how many times they hear it.

"It" is Calling the Hogs. Arkansas fans do it several times per game, whether the event is football, basketball, or even baseball. They do it at Razorback Club meetings. They do it at pep rallies before away games and at bowl or tournament sites. What does it sound like? It is "*Whooooooooo, Piiigg, Sooooooooooey!*" To do it properly, it is screamed three times, then followed by "*Razorbacks!*"

It has caused plenty of commotion. When Arkansas fans took over Dallas in the old Southwest Conference basketball tournament days, Texans would moan at the frequency of the cheer—particularly when the Razorbacks would thump their SWC opponents on the way to another championship. Arkansas won the last three SWC Tournaments (9–0) it played in. Think other SWC fans dreaded hearing the Hog Call after hearing it so many times?

It caused quite a stir in Arkansas' first year in the Southeastern Conference, too. When the UA basketball team arrived in the arena in Birmingham for its first ever SEC Tournament contest, nearly

7,000 Razorbacks fans erupted in a Hog Call. Another game was going on at the time but fans in the arena stopped, stunned to hear that Kentucky had a challenger in fan support.

The Call began sometime in the 1920s; no one is quite sure when. Supposedly Arkansas was trailing in a game when a pig farmer in the crowd started imitating the way he would call his own hogs. Other fans picked up on it. Legend has it the Razorbacks rallied for a victory and the call became an immediate hit.

Whether the same farmer appeared at the next game is unknown, but the cheer continued. It eventually evolved into the call it is today. Whether it is 70,000 fans at Reynolds Razorback Stadium, 20,000 at Bud Walton, 10,000 at Baum Stadium, or two Arkansans who meet each other somewhere outside of the state, Razorbacks fans love calling the Hogs.

27 Brittenum to Crockett

Texas was ranked No. 1 and Arkansas No. 3 when the Longhorns came to Fayetteville in October 1965. Texas had been national champion in 1963. The Razorbacks defeated the 'Horns in 1964 and won the post-bowl national title. In fact, Texas' only loss in its previous 26 games had been to Arkansas. And the Hogs entered the game on a 16-game winning streak. Suffice it to say, there were a lot of emotions on both sides leading up to the contest.

The game couldn't have started better for the Razorbacks. Blasted by Jim Williams, Phil Harris of Texas fumbled a booming 58-yard punt by Bobby Nix and Martine Bercher dove on the ball in the UT end zone for an Arkansas touchdown. Texas was driving for the tying score when Harris fumbled again, this time into the

Jon Brittenum (15) passes to Bobby Crockett (83), who gets out of bounds at the Texas 1 to set up Brittenum's game-winning quarterback sneak against Texas in 1965.

arms of Tommy Trantham, who raced 77 yards for a score. And when Jon Brittenum hit Bobby Crockett with an 11-yard TD pass in the second quarter, the Hogs found themselves leading 20–0.

But the Longhorns were far from finished. They shut down the high-powered Razorback offense and eventually gained a 24–20 fourth-quarter lead. With time left for one last drive, Arkansas started on its own 20-yard line.

"When we got the ball back, the 20–0 lead seemed like a long time ago," recalled Crockett. "There was only a little more than four minutes left. We knew it would be our last chance to win.

Coach Broyles asked me if I could get open. I thought I could. He told me they would throw it to me all the way down the field."

And that's exactly what happened. Brittenum-to-Crockett accounted for 68 of the 80 yards on the game-winning drive. The Hogs landed at the Texas 11 before Crockett's final catch of the game.

"We kept running the same pattern," said Crockett. "The catches were pretty ordinary. It was throwing and catching, just like in practice. The only difference was it was happening in the biggest game of the year."

From the 11, Brittenum's pass was near the sideline, but Crockett managed to catch it in bounds before sliding out at the 1. For all the catches Crockett made in his Arkansas career, that acrobatic grab at the Longhorns 1 is the one for which he is most remembered. Brittenum snuck into the end zone on the next play and Arkansas intercepted a pass on Texas' final possession to complete one of the Hogs' most memorable victories ever in Razorback Stadium.

While the defense deserved much of the credit, it was Brittenum-to-Crockett that got the glory as the Razorbacks kept their winning streak alive. When it was all over, legendary announcer Lindsey Nelson, who did the play-by-play for NBC's telecast of the game, said to his audience, "That was the greatest game I've ever worked."

28 Stoerner to Lucas

Clint Stoerner waited a year for retribution. But he almost had to wait a lifetime. It finally happened for him in the fourth quarter of Arkansas' 1999 game against Tennessee. And it was one of the sweetest moments of his life.

The 1998 Razorbacks were 8–0 when they visited Tennessee in Knoxville. The Vols were also undefeated, and ranked No. 1 in the country. Arkansas had begun the season, Houston Nutt's first as head coach, unranked, and it took eight weeks for the Hogs to climb to No. 10.

Arkansas led nearly the entire game and stopped Tennessee on a fourth-down play near midfield with less than two minutes to play. All the Razorbacks had to do was run out the clock to preserve their lead. And even if the Hogs had to punt, it would leave the Vols with little time to overcome Arkansas' 24–21 advantage.

But disaster struck as Stoerner, the UA quarterback, stepped on offensive guard Brandon Burlsworth's ankle, slipped, and fumbled the football. Tennessee recovered, scored a touchdown, and used the victory over Arkansas as a stepping stone toward an ultimate national championship.

Stoerner was devastated. It had still been a great season for Arkansas, but the Hogs spent the off-season pondering what might have been. By the time the Razorbacks met Tennessee in Fayetteville in 1999, they were not in the top 10; the Volunteers, on the other hand, were ranked third in the country and were hoping to repeat as national champs.

But there was plenty of motivation fueling the Hogs' fire. "It was an intense week for me," Stoerner recalled. "I shared a lot of what I was feeling that week but held back some. I never wanted to win a game more than I wanted to win that one."

Arkansas grabbed the early lead but found themselves trailing 24–14 in the third quarter. Late in the third quarter, Stoerner hit Boo Williams with a deep pass for a touchdown to trim the Vols advantage to three points.

Midway through the fourth quarter, Arkansas marched to the Tennessee 23. In the huddle Stoerner changed the call sent in from

Nutt. He called for a route that had Anthony Lucas, his favorite target, headed for the end zone. The gambit worked. Stoerner's strike found Lucas for the go-ahead touchdown.

Tennessee drove to the Arkansas 10 with its final possession but the Razorbacks held. The Vols missed on four straight passes, and Stoerner only had to take a knee to secure the victory.

"The year before, I felt like I let my teammates, our fans, and the entire state down," Stoerner said. "When Anthony made that catch it was like a huge weight being lifted off of me. It was an emotional moment. It is still emotional for me years later."

Ironically, the score was the same as the year before—28–24—but the outcome, of course, was different. It was an early game, scheduled for television, and the sellout crowd stayed and celebrated. They tore down the goal posts and carried one of them all the way to Dickson Street.

29 Miracle on Markham

Arkansas was just 8–3 when it hosted LSU at War Memorial Stadium in the 2002 regular-season finale. However, there was a lot on the line: the winner of the UA-LSU game would be the Western Division's representative in the SEC Championship Game in Atlanta.

Matt Jones, a spectacular runner and decent passer, had quarterbacked the Razorbacks into position to play for the Western Division title, but the Tigers had contained him most of the day. Jones had completed only two of his 13 passes when the Hogs took over at their own 19 with just 40 seconds left to play.

"I was having a terrible game," Jones conceded. "I couldn't hit anything."

Many in the sellout crowd had left the stadium before the Razorbacks started their final march. There wasn't much hope. Fred Talley had scored on a long touchdown run to narrow LSU's lead to 17–14 but the Tigers marched the length of the field to a field goal that made it 20–14. There wasn't enough time left to give Talley the ball again.

So with less than a minute remaining, the Razorbacks were starting down a six-point deficit and a long 81 yards. Jones never appeared rattled on the football field, no matter what the circumstances. He annoyed coach Houston Nutt by humming while the coach gave him last-second instructions going into the last position. But Nutt wasn't nearly as annoyed as the Tigers by the time the game was finished.

On first down, Jones found Richard Smith, whose defender had fallen down, for a 50-yard gain to the LSU 31. An incompletion stopped the clock. Jones' primary target on the next play was George Wilson, but he was covered. Option No. 2 was Smith—nope, he was covered, too. Also well defended was third option Sparky Hamilton.

Protected magnificently by his offensive line, Jones heaved the ball into the end zone in the direction of DeCori Birmingham, whose primary responsibility on the play was to serve as a decoy and take the safety out of the play. Birmingham actually drew double coverage, but he leaped at just the right time and came down with the football.

"LSU was really good on defense but all day long the receivers were asking Coach Nutt to give us a shot," Birmingham recalled. "We believed we were better than LSU's defensive backs. When Richard made the first catch, we knew we had a chance.

"Matt was scrambling when I ran into the end zone. I saw him throw the ball up. When I watched the play later I saw there were two defenders right there, but while I was focusing on the ball, I didn't even see them. I was in the back of the end zone and just happened to jump at the right time. The next thing I knew, everyone was jumping on top of me."

The many fans who were still in the stadium exploded with jubilation. Razorbacks players celebrated, too. Unfortunately, the celebration turned excessive in the eyes of the officials and David Carlton was forced to attempt the tie-breaking extra point from 15 yards farther away.

Nonetheless, Carlton kicked the ball through the uprights with just nine seconds remaining. With an unlikely completion, Arkansas had gone from what appeared to be a disappointing loss to a SEC Western Division championship.

The pass from Jones to Birmingham was dubbed "the Miracle on Markham,"—named after the street that runs just outside the stadium—and it will forever be one of the most memorable moments in Razorback history.

30 Ken Hatfield's Punt Return

After a disappointing 5–5 season in 1963, Arkansas was a heavy underdog when it went to Austin in 1964 to face the defending national champion and top-ranked Texas Longhorns.

"Texas had won 14 in a row and was ranked No. 1," recalled Ken Hatfield. "We were the upstarts. We were 4–0 but hadn't dominated anybody. They had a great punter in Ernie Koy, who was also a great back. Opponents averaged less than three yards a return against them. In the paper the morning of the game the sportswriter guaranteed there would be no significant punt return

Ken Hatfield returns a punt 81 yards for Arkansas' first touchdown in its 1964 win at Texas.

against Texas that night." That was a lofty guarantee since Hatfield had led the nation in punt returns as a junior and was on his way to doing it again in 1964, his senior season.

The game was scoreless when Hatfield made a play that has been regarded as one of the top plays in Razorbacks history. "I caught the ball at our 19-yard line and I knew right away they had kicked it too far," said Hatfield. "I knew we could block them. Jim Lindsey threw the first block. When I went to the wall on the sideline, our whole team was there. I ran right by our bench and our players knocked down eight Texas players. Somewhere around the Texas 35 or 40, Jerry Lamb knocked Koy off balance.

"I've seen that play on film several times, and I sure look slow, but the play went 81 yards and put us ahead. Our fans were ecstatic and so were we. That play gave us great confidence and we definitely believed we would win the game."

And the Hogs did win it. The final was 14–13, with Hatfield's punt return the highlight. The Razorbacks won the rest of their games on the schedule that year, and ultimately the post-bowl national championship. It can be said that none of what Arkansas accomplished in 1964 would have been possible had it not been for Hatfield's punt return against Texas.

31 Tailgating at War Memorial Stadium

Tailgating on the golf course surrounding War Memorial Stadium is one of the great traditions of Razorbacks football and a must-do for any Razorbacks fan. In fact, it is almost a sport unto itself. There are many fans who tailgate all day. Some don't even enter the stadium for the game. Instead they remain in their tailgating positions, enjoying a variety of foods and beverages while watching the game on television and listening to radio broadcasts.

Of course, watching a game on TV while on the golf course wasn't possible when Razorbacks fans began tailgating around the stadium so many years ago. But fans have been assembling outside War Memorial for decades, proving Arkansas fans were ahead of their time. Tailgating is now a huge pastime at nearly every college stadium but it was popular in Little Rock long before it became a national trend.

As other stadiums have increased in size, Arkansas' home away from home has remained at a little more than 53,000. Tailgating on the golf course remains one of the most charming aspects of games at War Memorial Stadium, and a great reason to keep games there. Few venues in the Southeastern Conference have as much tailgating space available so close to the stadium. Hogs fans attending the game don't have to walk far from their tailgating location to their entry points at War Memorial.

Fans from central and south Arkansas covet the tradition of playing at War Memorial Stadium. When he became athletic director, John Barnhill recognized the importance of playing games in the capital city as a means of building statewide loyalty. Before Interstates 40 and eventually 549 made Fayetteville more accessible, Little Rock was the central place where all Arkansans could gather in the shortest period of time. In the 1940s, '50s and '60s, it took nearly six hours to drive from Little Rock to Fayetteville.

The Hogs played their Little Rock games at Quigley Stadium in the early 1940s. Barnhill said the city needed a new stadium if Arkansas were to continue to play there. War Memorial Stadium was built in time for the 1948 season and was superior to Razorback Stadium for many years. In fact, during Arkansas' most glorious decade in football, the 1960s, the Hogs frequently played more home games per season in Little Rock than Fayetteville.

Access to Fayetteville and the switch to the Southeastern Conference forced UA athletic officials to move more games to the UA campus, but the Razorbacks are contracted to play at War Memorial at least through 2018. That means there will be plenty of future opportunities to turn the War Memorial Golf Course into a huge Razorbacks party.

Clyde Scott

Most of the credit for Arkansas' rise to national significance in college football rightfully goes to Frank Broyles. But the beginning of the Razorbacks' football renaissance was marked by the enrollment of Clyde Scott in time for the 1946 season.

Scott played two years at Navy during World War II, where he was one of the best players in the country. When the war ended, he was free to transfer. A native of Smackover, Arkansas, he picked UA and first-year coach John Barnhill. And there was a factor involved that was far greater than Scott's attachment to his home state. He met and married Leslie Hampton, who had been Miss Arkansas in 1944.

Scott had three fabulous seasons as a tailback and defensive back. As a senior at Arkansas, he rushed for 1,463 yards, averaging 7.1 yards per carry. He helped the Hogs earn a Southwest Conference title in 1946 and saved a 0–0 tie with LSU in the Cotton Bowl with a clutch fourth-down tackle at the UA 1-yard line.

Three times an All-Southwest Conference selection, Scott had a memorable year in 1948. First he finished second in the 110-yard hurdles at the Olympic Games in London. Then he earned All-America honors for his football heroics during the '48 season.

Barnhill's regime was cemented by Scott's decision to become a Razorback. The Hogs were barely competitive in the decade preceding that 1946 season. Their tailback's speed was simply amazing. As a track and field star, he tied the world record in the 110 hurdles when he beat Northwestern's Bill Porter for the NCAA championship (only to be nudged by Porter at the Olympics).

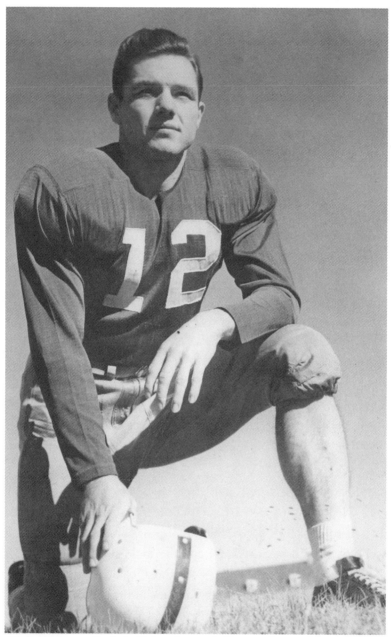

Clyde Scott was a football All-American and Olympic silver medalist in the same year.

The Greatest Athlete

Who was the greatest athlete in Razorbacks history? That question would be the cause of great debate. Many would argue for Clyde Scott, who in 1948 won a silver medal in the Olympic Games and was named an All-American in Razorbacks football.

You could certainly make a case for Lance Alworth, too. The fleet receiver twice led the nation in punt returns, played on the UA baseball team, and also lettered in track.

When it was more common to play more than one sport, Wear Schoonover was a star in football and basketball for the Razorbacks. He was an All-American in football in 1929 and also helped the Razorbacks win the Southwest Conference title in basketball.

It would be hard to make a case against Mike Conley, though. He could have played any sport but flourished in track. Surprisingly, his track career didn't start, though, until he tried out for basketball.

"He could have been a [basketball] starter if he had stayed with it," Eddie Sutton said at the time. "He had the potential to be a very good player. We told him his future was in track, though."

Conley's brother Steve, an all-SEC defensive end for the Razorbacks in 1995 said, "Mike's best sport in high school may have been football. He would have been a great college receiver."

In the end, Conley made a good decision. Not only did he win 16 NCAA championships in the long and triple jumps, he earned a silver medal, then a gold, at the Olympics. He also won the Foot Locker Dunking Championship three times, competing against some pretty darn good athletes.

"Scott was the fastest man I ever saw in a uniform," Barnhill once told longtime sportswriter Orville Henry. "The uniform never seemed to slow him down. He was also the best defensive back I ever had. Even if he made a mistake, he could cover it up."

Scott played in the NFL with the Philadelphia Eagles and Detroit Lions before a knee injury forced him to retire. He became a very successful businessman in central Arkansas following his football career.

Barnhill had Scott's No. 12 retired. It is one of just two football numbers ever retired by the school.

33 Lance Alworth

Numbers will never tell the true value of Lance Alworth as an Arkansas Razorback. While his numbers were good, he twice led the NCAA in punt returns, and his presence on campus gave instant credibility to Frank Broyles' program.

Alworth was from Mississippi. He was the type of native son who always went to Ole Miss, where Johnny Vaught had a national power that annually competed for the national championship. But there was one problem: Alworth was married, and Vaught had a policy against having married players.

Broyles, well aware, took advantage. He courted Lance not only but his father. They played golf together. He did everything he could think of to convince the Alworths that Arkansas was about to become a strong program. By the time Vaught told the Alworths he would make an exception to his policy, it was too late. Alworth was already a Razorback.

While the Hogs finished just 4–6 in 1958, Broyles' first year, the freshman team, featuring Alworth and a slew of other talented players, was sensational. By the time Alworth went through spring practice in preparation for his sophomore season, it was obvious he would be special.

"During spring practice in 1959 a player came to my office and said, 'Mr. Cheyne, I've just been practicing with Arkansas' next All-American,'" said then sports information director Bob Cheyne. "It was Lance Alworth.

"Lance had great speed. In an intrasquad track meet he ran a 9.4 in the 100-yard dash. That was a world record at the time. And he ran 9.6 several times. A defender who tried to cover him had his hands full. The guy ran with his knees high, like a great

Big Hands

Jim Benton had a huge pair of hands. Perhaps that's why he was way ahead of his time in terms of being a college football wide receiver. His coach, Fred Thomsen, believed in the passing game and had a pair of excellent passing quarterbacks, Jack Robbins and Dwight "Paddlefoot" Sloan from 1935 to 1937. Kay Eakin joined the group in 1937 and played in '38 and '39 as well. The favorite receiver for all three of them was Benton.

The receiver's hands would swallow those of an average man with a handshake, and they were perfect for catching footballs. During the 1936 and '37 seasons he caught 83 passes for 1,303 yards and 13 touchdowns. Those numbers may not sound enormous by today's standards, but they were unusually high for the period. Indeed, his career receiving yards remained a school record for more than three decades, before it was finally broken by Chuck Dicus. And Benton's UA single-season record of 814 receiving yards—which was also an NCAA record at the time—stood another year before being claimed by Mike Reppond.

Benton went on to an All-Pro career in the NFL. He spent eight years with the Cleveland / Los Angeles Rams and one with the Chicago Bears and played on two NFL championship teams. He led the NFL in receiving yards in 1945 and 1946—including a remarkable 303-receiving-yard game, an NFL record that stood for 40 years—and made 288 career catches for 4,801 yards. At the time of his retirement, he ranked second on the NFL career receiving yardage list. He is also a member of the Pro Football Hall of Fame's All-1940s Team.

racehorse. He had everything you would want in a great running back."

Alworth ran, caught passes, and generally disrupted defenses. His teams won 25 games and three Southwest Conference championships during his three years of eligibility. He also ran track and played baseball.

Broyles remembered one of Alworth's plays as one of the best he ever witnessed. In Alworth's sophomore season, Arkansas trailed

SMU 14–13 after scoring a late touchdown. With a SWC title on the line, Broyles decided to go for two. Alworth got the call.

"Lance kept spinning off of tacklers and finally made it into the end zone," Broyles said. "I couldn't tell you how many tackles he broke. It was only three yards, but was one of the greatest runs I've ever seen."

The two-point conversion and a late safety gave the Razorbacks a 17–14 win that led to Broyles' first conference championship.

"He was tough," Cheyne recalled. "Obviously, Ole Miss was mad because they didn't get him. We played them one year in Memphis and they were determined to knock him out of the game by whatever means necessary. But after they hit him he kept bouncing up. They couldn't knock him out."

Alworth's college career ended after the Hogs lost to Alabama in the Sugar Bowl following the 1961 season. He became the subject of a bidding war between the National Football League and the fledgling American Football League. The AFL considered it a coup when Alworth signed with the San Diego Chargers. He played nine seasons with the Chargers before joining the Dallas Cowboys for the final two years of his career, and was one of the greatest wide receivers in pro football history. Nicknamed "Bambi"—perhaps because of his unique running style—he helped the Cowboys win a championship with a touchdown reception against the Miami Dolphins in Super Bowl VI.

34 Pat Summerall

Originally from Florida, an NFL standout with the New York Giants, and one of the best known NFL announcers of all time, it's easy to forget that Pat Summerall, a collegian so long ago, was a Razorbacks football player.

Summerall grew up in Lake City, Arkansas, about 1,000 miles from Fayetteville. He earned his scholarship when one of John Barnhill's assistants, line coach Hobert Hooser, set up a tryout camp at Summerall's high school. Fortunately for Arkansas, Hooser was a former coach at Lake City, and Summerall's father knew of him.

"Arkansas was on a roll in football then," Summerall wrote in his autobiography, which was published a few years before he passed away. "They had been to bowl games in the previous two years, so I signed on the dotted line to become a Hog on full scholarship."

Unfortunately, there were no bowl games during Summerall's tenure. He played for Barnhill in 1949, then Otis Douglas in 1950 and '51. The Razorbacks were 5–5 in '49 and '51 and 2–8 in 1950 despite having such future pros as Fred Williams, Lamar McHan, Lew Carpenter, Floyd Sagely, Bob Griffin, Dave Hanner, and Buddy Sutton. Another of Summerall's teammates, briefly, was Miller Barber, who later became a terrific professional golfer after a standout career in the sport as an undergraduate.

"I went to Arkansas on a football scholarship and remember some of the scrimmages we had," Barber said before he passed away. "Pat and I were in the same class, and as freshmen we would get chewed up by the varsity. I remember one scrimmage when I had blood all over my face and I had both hands on my knees in the huddle. I told the guys, 'I don't know about the rest of you but I'm gonna find me another sport.'"

The switch was obviously great for Barber. Summerall, on the other hand, stuck it out. He loved Fayetteville and didn't mind being so far from home except during the first difficult winter he encountered. He told Barnhill he didn't have a winter coat, so the

Razorback athletic director introduced him to Jack Stephens, a wealthy investment banker who took Summerall to Dillard's and bought him one.

"It was the beginning of a great friendship," said Summerall, who later did the telecast of the Masters golf tournament. Stephens was for several years the chairman at the Augusta National Golf Club in Georgia, the course where the Masters is played.

Summerall played tight end (there were no wideouts in many offenses back then), defensive end, and became the place kicker for three years for the Razorbacks. The Hogs didn't kick many field goals back then, but one he kicked made him an instant hero throughout the state.

Arkansas was 2–2 when fourth-ranked and unbeaten Texas came to Razorback Stadium in 1951. At that point, the Razorbacks had never beaten the Longhorns in Fayetteville. Shortly before halftime Summerall kicked a short field goal to give the Hogs a 9–7 lead. When the teams traded touchdowns in the second half and the game ended in a 16–14 Razorbacks victory, Summerall's field goal ended up being the difference. It was just the third field goal of his career.

"The celebration lasted for days," Summerall said. "That field goal cemented my place in Razorback history."

Indeed, that was the highlight for Summerall at Arkansas. He went on to much bigger moments in the NFL, mostly with the Giants. And his broadcasting career was amazing. He teamed with John Madden for what most experts believe was the best NFL broadcasting team in history.

But there was one more highlight for Summerall at Arkansas. He remained a close, lifetime friend of Sagely, who had a successful business in Fort Smith. When Arkansas prepared to celebrate its football centennial in 1994, Broyles asked Sagely if he could convince Summerall to narrate a video documenting the history of the Razorbacks.

"Floyd made the contact and Pat very graciously agreed to do it," Broyles said. "He wouldn't let us pay him. He did a wonderful job and the video, with Pat's narration, was a treasure for Razorback fans."

35 Montgomery to Dicus

After a disappointing 4–5–1 season in 1967, Arkansas turned to a youth movement in 1968—and it paid off big time. Sophomores Bill Montgomery (quarterback), Bill Burnett (tailback), and Chuck Dicus (wide receiver) became instant starters, and the Razorbacks offense took off. On the other side of the ball, linebacker Cliff Powell and defensive lineman Dick Bumpas led a defense that was loaded with underclassmen.

The Hogs romped to a 9–1 regular season, losing only to Texas. For the third time in the decade of the '60s, the Razorbacks were invited to the Sugar Bowl. The opponent was fourth-ranked Georgia, the Southeastern Conference champion with the odd record of 8–0–2.

Georgia's defense was ranked the best in the country. Safety Jake Scott—who later started for the Miami Dolphins' undefeated team that went on to become Super Bowl champion—was a consensus All-American who would have the responsibility of trying to stop Dicus, whose reputation was growing and would lead to All-America recognition in 1969 and 1970.

"Georgia's defense was exceptional," said Dicus. "They relied heavily on man-to-man coverage. They could afford to because their cornerbacks were outstanding and Jake Scott was the best safety in the country. But our coaches had a passing game plan

Chuck Dicus (20) beats Georgia All-American Jake Scott (13) for the game's only touchdown in Arkansas' 1969 Sugar Bowl victory over Georgia.

based on using me in the slot formation. Georgia had not seen much of that during the season. It worked well for us."

As it turned out, it was the Arkansas defense that dominated. And Scott and the Bulldogs had no answer for Dicus. After a scoreless first quarter, Montgomery hit Dicus in full stride for a 27-yard touchdown on the first play of the second stanza. It would remain the only touchdown of the entire game. But it wasn't the last time Montgomery and Dicus connected.

By the time the final horn sounded, Montgomery had hit Dicus 12 times for 169 yards and Bob White had kicked three field goals; Georgia's only score came on a safety. The Razorbacks finished seventh in the final Associated Press poll after the 16–2 victory.

"It was exciting to be named the game's most valuable player but it was really our defense that won the game," Dicus said. "Our defense recovered five fumbles and intercepted three passes. They stopped Georgia all day."

Yes, the defense was outstanding, but it was Montgomery and Dicus who grabbed the national spotlight that day. They retained it throughout the next two seasons.

Barry Switzer, Jimmy Johnson, and Pete Carroll

Only three coaches in history have led college teams to national championships and NFL teams to Super Bowl titles. All three have ties to Arkansas.

Jimmy Johnson was the first to accomplish the double feat. He was a 198-pound nose guard on Arkansas' 1964 national championship team and later served as defensive coordinator on Frank Broyles' coaching staff. After a stint as head coach at Oklahoma State, Johnson became head coach at Miami, where he led the Hurricanes to the national title in 1987.

When Jerry Jones, a teammate of Johnson's at Arkansas, bought the Dallas Cowboys, he hired Johnson to replace the legendary Tom Landry as coach. After a rough start, Johnson restored the Cowboys to greatness. Dallas won back-to-back Super Bowls in 1993 and 1994, easily defeating Buffalo both times.

Barry Switzer, who co-captained Broyles' first Southwest Conference co-championship team in 1959, later joined the Hogs coaching staff and tutored receivers during Arkansas' 22-game winning streak in 1964 and 1965. He left to become a member of Jim McKenzie's staff at Oklahoma, and was an assistant for several years before becoming head coach.

Switzer had a legendary career with the Sooners, guiding them to national championships in 1974, 1975, and 1985. Years later, after Johnson had delivered two Super Bowl championships to Dallas, Johnson and Jones had a strained relationship. Johnson left and Jones replaced him with Switzer. It didn't take Switzer long to guide the Cowboys to another NFL title. They beat Pittsburgh in the Super Bowl in the coach's second season.

Pete Carroll's Arkansas connection isn't as strong as that of Johnson's and Switzer's, but his year with the Razorbacks made an impression. He was a graduate assistant on Lou Holtz's 1977 staff. And since his only previous experience as a coach was at Pacific, Arkansas was Carroll's first contribution to a big-time program.

He came at the right time, serving under Holtz and defensive coordinator Monte Kiffin. The Razorbacks went 11–1, whipped Oklahoma in the Orange Bowl, and finished third in the country.

Carroll has made quite a few stops in his coaching career, including the New York Jets and New England Patriots as head coach, before heading back to the collegiate ranks as head coach at Southern California. Hard as it may be to believe today, the program was then in disrepair and in desperate need of reconstruction. Carroll worked his magic and USC was restored as a national power. He led the Trojans to two national titles, then decided to accept the head coaching position with the Seattle Seahawks. Seattle also needed reconstruction, and Carroll did it again, eventually taking the Seahawks to a Super Bowl victory over Denver to complete the 2013 season.

"The only coaches to ever win national championships and Super Bowl championships are part of Razorback football history," Broyles said. "We are quite proud of that."

37 Orville Henry

No one ever has or ever will know as much about Razorbacks football as Orville Henry. Named sports editor of the *Arkansas Gazette* when he was just a teenager, he decided after World War II that the Razorbacks were the biggest sports story in the state and that he would cover them appropriately.

Henry wrote about John Barnhill, Otis Douglas, Bowden Wyatt, and Jack Mitchell, but his greatest days were covering Frank Broyles during Broyles' 19 years as head football coach. He was the only journalist from central Arkansas who made frequent trips to Fayetteville before the roads made the trip a little easier in the 1970s. He and Broyles became great friends while Henry documented the greatest era of sustained national prominence in UA history.

"I was overly impressed by how Orville Henry could sit at a typewriter in the press box or back in his office in Little Rock and peck away with his fingers a million miles an hour," said Bob Cheyne, who worked with Henry for more than 20 years in his role as sports information director. "He always was one of the last to leave the press box after the game. He took covering a game as his most important job. He would always want the statistics we would give him to reinforce what he was going to say.

"Orville was one of the most splendid guys I've ever known in sports. He loved to write Arkansas pregame and game stories. He knew the facts and the figures, but he sought the advice of Frank [Broyles] or some of the key players to support what he thought was the truth about a game or a play."

Broyles noted, "Orville would pick me up at the airport every Sunday when I would fly down to do my television show. We would have lunch and talk about the previous day's game. He was very thorough. He didn't want to just write his opinion. He wanted to know what I thought."

Cheyne added, "When people read his columns, they knew he could be trusted. He was admired. He told it as it was, without any negatives about a coach. He had the most readable page in the Southwest Conference. Obviously, he was biased because he covered the Razorbacks for the *Gazette*, but he wasn't a 'homer,' and the other coaches in the league knew it. He could talk to any coach in the conference and get what he wanted. I had great respect for Orville."

Henry covered the Razorbacks for more than 50 years. Along with his legacy of journalism, he also wrote, with Jim Bailey, *The Razorbacks: A History of Arkansas Football.* The book, whose last edition was published in 1996, remains the standard for Razorbacks history up to that point. Beano Cook, who spent the last four decades of his life working for ABC, then ESPN, once said, "Orville Henry has written more about the Razorbacks than Carl Sandberg has about Abraham Lincoln."

As the *Arkansas Gazette* was faltering, Henry switched to the *Arkansas Democrat*. The move was a death knell for the *Gazette*. Henry later moved to Stephens Media, where he worked until he became too ill to write.

When Arkansas renovated the Broyles Athletic Center and decided to include a museum, Henry was summoned. Because of his numerous contacts with former Razorbacks, he was hired to collect artifacts and write much of the copy that still remains in the facility today.

Henry's death in 2002 brought sadness to an entire state that grew up enjoying his incredibly thorough columns and stories about the Razorbacks.

38 Bob Cheyne

Bob Cheyne was Arkansas' first sports information director. He began his sports journalism career as a student, covering the Razorbacks for the *Northwest Arkansas Times* for one year. He then became the university's SID in 1948. He was a pioneer in the profession.

When Cheyne took the job, there were no statistical records, and the position was not always given full respect. "We used to travel by train," Cheyne recalled. "Our trainer would make travel arrangements. Sometimes he would include me, sometimes he wouldn't. They didn't recognize the value of what we later called a sports information director. I never knew if I would have a bed or not. There were some trips where I would just sit up all night. I

Bob Cheyne was sports information director for 22 years and "Voice of the Razorbacks" for a decade.

would have a meal in the morning, but didn't have a good night's sleep."

Gradually, things got better in the travel department. Still, putting together Arkansas' first brochures was a different story. "I went to the lower, lower floor of the university library to see if they had any information on athletics, and they did," Cheyne said. "They would take me down there and close me in with a phone. I would read and take notes; they wouldn't let me take anything home, so I had to do all the work there.

"Also I contacted the wives of John C. Futrall, the first football coach and later UA president, and Francis Schmidt, who coached football and basketball in the 1920s. After we had a relationship, they gave me access to documents they still had, including some from as early as the 1890s. I always returned the documents after making copious notes.

"Gradually, I put everything together into brochures. I loved the work. It was like going back and living history." Indeed, Cheyne has been Arkansas' greatest sports historian. Without his efforts, many rich details in Razorbacks athletics would have been lost to history forever.

Cheyne worked with John Barnhill, Otis Douglas, Bowden Wyatt, Jack Mitchell, and Frank Broyles during their respective tenures as Razorbacks football coaches. Barnhill was the athletic director for each of the 21 years Cheyne worked as SID. Just before the 1958–59 basketball season began, Cheyne added Voice of the Razorbacks to his list of duties.

"Wally Ingalls had been the radio play-by-play man but had a disagreement with the manager of the radio station where he worked," Cheyne said. "He left the station, and a week later he was out as the Razorback voice as well. John Barnhill asked me if I could do it since I knew the players so well. I said yes."

Cheyne did football and basketball play-by-play for nearly a decade before Barnhill summoned him again. "I loved doing the games and tried to keep the broadcast from being one-sided," Cheyne said. "Even our opponents felt they could trust me. But Barney thought the Voice of the Razorbacks should be connected to the central part of the state. He called me in his office and asked me to write a letter to Bud Campbell, who was sports director at KATV in Little Rock, and tell him the university had selected him to do play-by-play of the games. At first I was deeply hurt, but I could see why Barnhill made the decision, so I was the one who informed Bud."

Cheyne remained SID for another two years before leaving the athletic department. He spent the rest of his working years in the private sector. But he never lost his zeal for the Razorbacks nor his love for Broyles, with whom he remained close friends.

"Frank and I both lost our wives," Cheyne said. "We can talk on the same level. My wife, Ginny, and his wife, Barbara, were very close friends. Frank and I have been through many of the same adversities."

As long as his health allowed him, Cheyne continued to attend Razorbacks athletic events. He remained the university's top historian, after discovering and documenting scores and statistics that had previously been forgotten, until his death in March 2014.

39 Corliss and Scotty

Most Razorbacks fans knew who Corliss Williamson was from the time he was in junior high. He already was doing the stuff of legend, such as shattering a backboard with a slam dunk—as an eighth grader. By the time he entered Russellville High School,

Terry and Tolson

Although they played before Eddie Sutton and Nolan Richardson brought great success to Razorbacks basketball, Martin Terry and Dean Tolson kept Arkansas fans entertained while playing for Lanny Van Eman's "Running Razorbacks."

The Razorbacks certainly ran, but so did their opponents. At times, the Hogs would score more than 100 points—but they might give up more than 100 as well. And that was before the three-point field goal was a part of the game!

Case in point: the scores of the last two games of Arkansas' 8–18 season in 1972, the first Terry and Tolson played together, were victories against Baylor and Rice: 131–109 and 113–108, respectively.

Terry averaged more points per game than any Razorback before or after. His average of 28.3 in 1973 is still a school record, as is his career average of 26.3. In just two years at Arkansas, after transferring from junior college, Terry scored 1,368 points in just 52 games.

Tolson played three years for Van Eman. He averaged 17 points per game and had a 22.5 scoring average in 1974, the year after Terry had finished. He also finished with 845 career rebounds, a figure that still ranks as fourth best at Arkansas. He also had 10 of the top 13 single-game rebounding efforts in school history.

Because they never played in the NCAA Tournament and their teams didn't win much, Terry and Tolson are frequently forgotten. But they were two of the best players in school history.

everyone in Arkansas was hoping Williamson would become a Razorback.

Few Razorbacks followers knew who Scotty Thurman was until he arrived on the UA campus. He was from a border state, Louisiana, but word was that only a few schools had been interested in him until late in the recruiting process. Arkansas coach Nolan Richardson, who liked Thurman from the beginning, convinced the young talent to enroll at the UA.

By the time Williamson and Thurman had played three years together at Arkansas, everyone who followed college basketball

Teammates Scotty Thurman (left) and Corliss Williamson (right) were 13–2 in NCAA tournament games. (AP Images)

knew who they were. Their credentials? They helped lead the Razorbacks to an 85–19 record, a national championship, an NCAA runner-up finish, and a Sweet Sixteen berth. Both players still rank among the school's top 10 career scorers. Williamson finished with 1,728 points; Thurman had 1,650 points.

Williamson's career scoring average of 19.0 is second only to that of Martin Terry. Thurman averaged 17.4 points per game in his first year, the highest scoring average ever posted by a freshman. Williamson averaged 20.4 points per game as a sophomore, the year Arkansas won the national championship. Thurman hit a school-record 102 three-point shots in 1995 and finished with a school-record career three-point percentage of .432.

"Our group did really well," said the always-understated Lee Mayberry, who played on four conference championship teams and squads that reached the NCAA Final Four and Elite Eight. "But Corliss and Scotty took it to another level. They won the national championship."

Corliss and Scotty didn't do it alone, but when the Razorbacks needed points, they were the two the team usually turned to. Even though he wasn't quite the 6'7" at which he was listed, Williamson dominated in the paint. Arkansas could always depend on him to score. His career field goal percentage was .583, fifth best in school history.

In 1995, when the Hogs were on the ropes against Memphis in the third round of the NCAA Tournament, they kept pounding it to Williamson, who almost single-handedly brought the Razorbacks from behind. Arkansas managed a tie at the end of regulation, won in overtime, and ultimately reached the national championship game. Williamson also was the Most Valuable Player of the Final Four, but it was Thurman who hit the shot everyone will always remember. With the shot clock about to hit zero, he launched a high-arching three-point attempt with less than a minute to go that snapped a 70–70 tie with Duke in the NCAA title game. The Blue Devils never recovered, and the Hogs won the national crown 76–72.

In the 1994 season alone, Thurman won three games with last-minute three-point shots. He did it at Tennessee, in overtime at LSU, and versus Duke. The following year, his field goal with fewer than 10 seconds left gave Arkansas a Bud Walton Arena victory over Kentucky. In all, Thurman hit the game-winning field goal in the last minute seven times.

During their time at Arkansas Thurman and Williamson became best friends.

"I met Corliss at an AAU 17-and-under tournament in Jonesboro," said Thurman. "We established a relationship. Neither of us knew we were going to Arkansas at that point. We joked about getting to the University of Arkansas together. I'm glad we did. He became the first really big man I ever got to play with.

"We shared a dorm room, then an apartment, our entire three years there. We talked about everything. We were different. He was the oldest in his family; I was the youngest in mine. Everyone knew who he was; I was a late bloomer."

Both bloomed at Arkansas. They won the national championship in a game attended by former President of the United States Bill Clinton, who of course was governor of Arkansas before he achieved the nation's highest office.

"We had a lot of highlights, but playing in front of the president and having the opportunity to speak in the Rose Garden after we won the national championship were great thrills," Thurman said.

40 MayDay

Lee Mayberry and Todd Day were both McDonald's All-Americans as seniors in high school, so even though Mayberry was from Tulsa and Day from Memphis, the two were already familiar with each other. They became best friends as teammates while at Arkansas.

"We went to Nike camps together and were in Fayetteville together during the summer before our freshman season," said Mayberry. "All these years later we are very close. When I go to Memphis, I stay at his home. When Todd's family comes to Tulsa, they stay with us."

Mayberry and Day not only spent four years together at Arkansas, they also were teammates with the Milwaukee Bucks for their first four seasons in the NBA. Both were drafted in the first round.

"Relationships are forever," Day said. "I've never met a better friend than Lee. To play four years with him at Arkansas, then four years in Milwaukee, was a blessing."

Mayberry and Day were indeed a blessing to Arkansas fans. Along with Oliver Miller, they were the ringleaders on teams that won four conference championships and earned a trip to the NCAA Final Four in 1990.

"Looking back, playing at Arkansas from 1988 to 1992 [were] the most fun four years of my life," said Mayberry. "The fans were amazing. They got behind you. They were our sixth man. Everywhere we played in the Southwest Conference, they were there. At the SWC Tournament in Dallas, it was always a sea of red. Arkansas is a different place. In that state, everybody likes the Razorbacks."

Day added, "When you play for the University of Arkansas, people never forget you. We had a Final Four reunion at Bud Walton in February of 2014. When we all walked into the arena, they all remembered us. It was a great day."

There was plenty to remember about Day, Mayberry, Miller, and their teammates. They helped earn the first SWC title won by coach Nolan Richardson at Arkansas, then won two more before switching to the Southeastern Conference. They won the SEC title, too, despite having a target on their chests.

"That first year in the SEC was fun," Mayberry said. "The SEC schools knew we had run through the SWC in our last three years there. They wanted us to know we were in a real league then. The SEC was the big dogs, and it wouldn't be easy to win. We felt we were just as good as any of the SEC schools and wanted to prove it."

Almost Seven Feet

George Kok was an awkward looking young man when he arrived on the University of Arkansas campus from Grand Rapids, Michigan, in the fall of 1944. He was almost seven feet tall (he officially measured 6'11") but didn't have much meat on his bones. He came to play basketball for the Razorbacks and coach Gene Lambert. At the time, there were few players his size at any weight.

In the 1940s, teams had to win a conference championship to qualify for an NCAA Tournament that hosted just eight teams. When Kok scored 22 points to help beat Oregon in 1945, the Razorbacks advanced to the Final Four. Unfortunately, there was another 6'11" standout in the college game. He was Bob Kurland at Oklahoma A&M (now State), a superb player who led the Cowboys to NCAA titles in 1945 and '46. It was his team that eliminated the Hogs in '45.

Kok and Kurland were matched against each other six times during those two years. Arkansas won just once, 41–38 at Little Rock. Kok never led the Razorbacks back to the Final Four, but his teams were 63–34 overall. By the time he was finished, Kok had scored 1,644 career points. It was by far a school record and it stood for 30 years before Marvin Delph broke it in 1978. With few defenders, other than Kurland, who could stop him, Kok had a career field goal percentage of .698. He averaged 17.5 points per game at a time when typical game scores were in the 40s.

The Razorbacks certainly proved how good they were—especially in winning both games against LSU, which was led by Shaquille O'Neal. The Razorbacks won at Baton Rouge when Day scored 43 points. To pull O'Neal away from the basket, Miller set up on the outside. And because Miller shot so well, O'Neal had to guard him. That left Day to post low on a smaller guard, and the 6'7" Day was unstoppable.

"I didn't get any sleep the night before the game," Day recalled. "I called my girlfriend, who is my wife now, and talked to her all night. I was still on a mission to prove myself. I had been suspended for the first semester that year and wanted to be a leader."

Day was the leader at Baton Rouge, and Mayberry stepped up in the rematch at Fayetteville. The Razorbacks trailed much of the game, but Mayberry kept his team close by hitting nine three-point field goals.

"That game was on one of the 'classic' channels not long ago," Mayberry said. "A buddy called and told me he watched me hit all those threes. We had to come from behind and win that game. In fact, we won in overtime."

During the four years Day, Mayberry, and Miller played together, the Razorbacks had a combined record of 115–24. Arkansas not only went to the Final Four in 1990 but also reached the Elite Eight in 1991 with one of the best teams in school history.

"We never won the national championship, but we paved the way for the team that came behind us," said Mayberry.

Day and Mayberry helped pave the way with lots of points. Day finished as Arkansas' career leading scorer, with 2,395 points. And only Day and Sidney Moncrief scored more than Mayberry's 1,940 points. Throw in Miller's 1,674 points, and the Hogs had three of their top 10 career scorers on the same team. Day's record still stands today.

"I never would have dreamed in a million years I would have become Arkansas' career scoring leader," Day said. "When I went to Arkansas, I played the game for fun. I never looked at myself as an NBA player. I couldn't imagine myself being on the same floor as someone like Michael Jordan. After a successful freshman year I realized the NBA would be possible. After my senior year, I was drafted by a team in the same division as Jordan and played against him eight times a year."

Although successful as pros, Day and Mayberry love to think about their time at Arkansas. Fans called for "MayDay" when they were Razorbacks. They are just as beloved more than two decades later.

41 Jon Richardson

As coach of the Missouri Tigers, Frank Broyles recruited the first African American football players ever to enroll at the university. He intended to do the same thing at the University of Arkansas when he became head coach in December 1957.

"I was told there was a Southwest Conference rule against integrating athletic teams," Broyles said. "I didn't like it, but there was nothing I could do."

It was a dozen more years before Broyles was able to recruit the first black athlete to play football at Arkansas—and he was a talented player. He was running back Jon Richardson from Little Rock.

"Jon was an outstanding running back," Broyles said. "His family certainly had a lot of decisions to make. But I'll never forget when Jon told me he was going to be a Razorback. We were so pleased and so proud."

Richardson came alone. His freshman class of 1969 was not eligible to play varsity football. (The NCAA did not allow freshmen to play until 1972.) But once he joined the varsity, he made an impact—especially as a kickoff returner. He had 780 yards on 35 returns during his career. The mark was a school record that stood for 10 years and still ranks among the top 10.

Bill Burnett was a record-breaking junior when Richardson enrolled. They were teammates in 1970 when Burnett was a senior and Richardson a sophomore. They roomed together on road trips.

"Jon was my backup," Burnett said. "That's why we roomed together. We were both involved in Fellowship of Christian Athletes, too, so that was another mutual engagement. I got to

Bill Burnett (33), Jon Richardson's mentor, scored 49 touchdowns during his Razorbacks career.

know Jon much better after both of us were through playing. He was a real fine young man. By and large he handled everything well.

"I'm sure there were some of those who gave him grief. I never saw or heard it, but I wouldn't have stood for it. Guys could see the writing on the wall. The time had come for our area of the country to have integrated teams."

Muskie Harris said Richardson's career and the integration that followed changed things dramatically. "I remember when black people would not call the Hogs," Harris said. "Now it's natural for all of us to call the Hogs together. One generation doesn't know what another generation went through. It wasn't all easy for Jon. He left twice, but wasn't gone long. His mother told him life was hard. Quitting was the easy way out. He needed to go back and do his job."

Because Richardson finished, others have followed. His numbers as a running back were good, not great, but the impact he left behind was enormous. "Jon was a quiet guy," said Harris, one of 13 African American football players in the freshman class of 1973. "I don't know if he was prepared to be a role model—I shared some great time together with [him] and his wife, Gloria—but how are you going to change if someone doesn't go through the door? Jon went through the door."

Harris said Richardson made it much easier for him and the other black athletes who followed. "Jon's last year was 1972, but Coach Broyles was smart," said Harris. "He kept Jon [on] to help recruit and take care of us. Wilson Matthews recruited Jon, and I was Coach Matthews' last recruit, so we had that in common. Jon guided us once we got there. I don't know if he had aspirations of playing once he finished his career with the Razorbacks, but all of us did. He let us know how difficult that would be. He told us they would help us academically, but we had to perform on the field. If we didn't perform, they would send us home. We were fearful of that. We all carried responsibility. We didn't want to be regarded as failures by our communities."

"When I started with FCA, I took Jon with me as often as possible because he was such an inspiration to the young, black athletes in our state," Burnett said. "He was an incredible ambassador and, like Jackie Robinson, he understood the role he was playing. I believe a lot of black athletes in our state became involved with FCA because of Jon, and I would guess most black athletes of all ages in Arkansas know who Jon Richardson was."

Richardson worked for years in northwest Arkansas before moving to Arizona, where he passed away.

Hogs on the Helmets

Emblems on football helmets are relatively new in the span of college football history. Until the 1950s, most teams wore helmets that had nothing at all on them. At Arkansas, they were dark leather until the late 1920s…when they became tan leather. In the 1930s, the Hogs wore white leather helmets adorned with cardinal wings as well as cardinal red leather with white wings.

In the mid-1940s, helmets went from leather to a shell. Arkansas' were white with a cardinal stripe. From 1952 to 1957, UA helmets were plain cardinal red. Face masks were added in 1956.

From 1958 through the 1963 season, Arkansas put white numbers on the sides of cardinal helmets. Longtime fans can still see Lance Alworth dodging tacklers with 23 emblazoned on his helmet. It was the style of the day. Alabama did it, too; in fact, Alabama still does it to this day.

Along the way, Frank Broyles wanted something unique on his team's helmets. After all, Arkansas is the only school with a razorback as its mascot. (Technically, Texarkana High School was actually the Razorbacks before the University of Arkansas, but by 1914 the UA had made the switch from originally being the Cardinals.)

Before the 1964 season, a hog decal was developed for Arkansas helmets. It was a big slobberknocker of a hog at that, much more cartoonish than the current hog. And that hog decal indeed set the Razorbacks apart. Any time Arkansas was on national television, the helmet was a distinguishing feature. It helped, too, that the Razorbacks were good. They won their first 21 games wearing the decal-clad helmets before ultimately losing to LSU in the Cotton Bowl.

Before the 1966 campaign, the Hog image was streamlined, and appeared much as it does today. The Razorback was slightly smaller and looked meaner, leaner, and more aggressive. From then until his the end of his coaching tenure in 1976, Frank Broyles left the hog on the helmet alone.

When Lou Holtz became coach, he wanted to do a few things that would distinguish his program from those in the past. Among them, he tinkered with the idea of changing the hog.

The mere thought of an outsider (Holtz had been head coach of North Carolina State, then the New York Jets, before coming to Arkansas) changing an Arkansas tradition infuriated Razorback fans. Holtz received plenty of opinions in his mailbox; few were favorable.

So the hog stayed the same. In later years it was enlarged slightly, but the shape has never varied. It is still unique. Arkansas is still the only university with a razorback as its mascot, and the hog on the helmet looks just as good today as it ever has.

43 Joe Ferguson

Arkansas was riding its most successful streak in history when the Razorbacks signed the No. 1 quarterback in the United States, Joe Ferguson, to a letter of intent in early 1969. Even before Ferguson enrolled in August, UA fans were anticipating how good the rifle-armed Shreveport, Louisiana, product would be.

Arkansas was coming off a 10–1 season in which it defeated Georgia in the Sugar Bowl, and hopes were high for the varsity in 1969. The Texas game had been moved from its normal slot in October to the first Saturday in December in order to accommodate an ABC telecast, in anticipation of what could be the game of the year in college football.

Interest was just as high in the freshman team because of Ferguson. Since freshmen weren't eligible to play for the varsity then, schools played a series of four or five games with their newcomers. At Arkansas the freshman squad was called "the Shoats."

"We had good quarterbacks throughout my first 10 years at Arkansas, but Joe Ferguson was the most highly regarded quarterback we had ever signed," said Frank Broyles. "He had a quick release and could zip the ball to his receivers quicker than any quarterback I'd ever seen."

In his book *The Razorbacks*, Orville Henry wrote, "Before he was out of high school, Joe Ferguson was a near-legendary figure in Louisiana and a blue chip recruit of national stature. Everybody wanted Joe. He opted for Arkansas because the Razorbacks had the closest winning program stressing pro-type passing techniques."

As expected, when Ferguson signed, so did excellent receivers like Jim Hodge, Mike Reppond, and Jack Ettinger. Another superb athlete was attracted to the offense as well. He was Jon Richardson, Arkansas' first African-American athlete. He came in the class of 1969 with Joe.

"I didn't know there were that many schools interested in me until after our high school season was over," Ferguson said. "My coach kept all the letters from me so I wouldn't be distracted. I received them from every major school: Texas, Tennessee, Michigan, and all the rest."

Ferguson considered Southern Cal, Texas, LSU, Alabama, and Arkansas. He and his dad determined that USC was too far away. Texas was running the wishbone, so the Longhorns were

Bruising a Chest

Passes got from Joe Ferguson's fingertips to his receivers' hands quicker than any Razorbacks quarterback in history—with the possible exception of Ryan Mallett, who quarterbacked the Hogs nearly four decades after Ferguson was finished. Yet after 18 years in the NFL and a few years of retirement, Ferguson could still bring it. He played in seven-on-seven charity games for Fellowship of Christian Athletes and Champions For Kids, firing passes to other former Razorbacks with the same zip he had in the early 1970s.

At one time, he lived next door to Stan Bedford, co-founder of Bedford Camera and Video, on Beaver Lake. Bedford, who has since passed away but was a few years younger than Ferguson, wanted to see what it was like to catch Joe's passes. On a Thanksgiving Day, he and some other neighbors, including Joe, staged a touch football game. "Stan was like a little kid," said Ferguson. "I'm not sure I've ever thrown to a more enthusiastic receiver." But Stan didn't know what he was getting into. "I couldn't catch the ball with my hands so it came all the way to my chest," Bedford said at the time. "After a few passes I had to quit. My chest was black and blue for weeks. I've never experienced anything like that."

When it looks easy for those NFL receivers, maybe it isn't quite so simple. Quarterbacks like Ferguson made gloves popular for NFL pass catchers.

eliminated. LSU was using a two-quarterback system. Eventually, it was Broyles and quarterback coach Don Breaux who persuaded Ferguson to choose Arkansas.

Ferguson became eligible for the varsity in 1970. Bill Montgomery, who had quarterbacked the Razorbacks to 19 victories in the previous two seasons, was a senior. Ferguson didn't want to redshirt, so he played behind Montgomery as backup.

"I always admired Bill," said Ferguson. "I could throw the ball better than he could but he was better in a lot of ways. It was a senior team, and he deserved to start."

Ferguson earned the starting nod in 1971 and didn't disappoint fans who had been waiting patiently to see the phenom play.

He passed for a school-record 2,203 yards, a mark that stood for 26 years until it was finally broken by Clint Stoerner (who Ferguson coached). The '71 Hogs started fast and looked like a lock for the Cotton Bowl after Ferguson passed Texas silly in a 31–7 rain-soaked win over the Longhorns at Little Rock.

"Texas always played one-on-one coverage," said Ferguson. "If you could beat them with the pass, that was it. Mike Reppond and Jim Hodge had the speed and experience to beat people. Mike got behind them for a 37-yard touchdown before halftime to give us a 21–7 lead and we were very confident after that."

However, on a night when Ferguson became the first Razorback to pass for more than 300 yards in a game, the Hogs lost to Texas A&M. A tie with Rice knocked Arkansas out of the Cotton Bowl running and into the Liberty Bowl, where it lost a controversial 14–13 game to Tennessee. Despite the loss, Ferguson was named the game's most valuable player.

Ferguson was the Heisman Trophy favorite in 1972, but it wasn't the season everyone thought it would be. Quarterback coach Breaux left for another position after the 1971 season and Ferguson was never utilized to his fullest capabilities. The season opened on a sour note with a Little Rock loss to USC, and the Hogs ended with a disappointing 6–5 record. Ferguson didn't start the season finale at Texas Tech.

Once the NFL came calling, Ferguson responded brilliantly. He played for 18 years, the first 12 in Buffalo. He is on the Buffalo Bills Wall of Fame.

When his pro career was over, Ferguson and his wife, Sandy, decided to move to northwest Arkansas. He served as sideline analyst for UA football broadcasts, then was hired by Danny Ford to coach quarterbacks. After Ford was fired, Houston Nutt retained Ferguson, who continued to coach Stoerner.

Since leaving coaching, Ferguson has been successful in real estate, working for former Razorback Jim Lindsey.

After all these years, Ferguson's throws are still legendary. Until Ryan Mallett became a Razorback nearly 40 years later, no Arkansas quarterback came close to matching Ferguson's velocity.

44 Frank vs. Darrell

Somehow, despite all logic, Frank Broyles and Darrell Royal were best friends. How in the world did that happen? Arkansas' biggest rival, by far, was Texas. And Broyles and Royal coached against each other 19 times from 1958 to 1976. So how could they get along so well?

"We both enjoyed a lot of the same things, particularly golf," Broyles explained. "When we were together, we never discussed the Arkansas-Texas football games. Well, we did once. He asked me about a game at War Memorial Stadium in Little Rock. He wanted to know if our phone wires had been crossed and were we picking up their communication. I told him yes.

"Then I asked him about a game at Austin, if they had stolen our signals. He said yes. That was it. We never discussed our games against each other again."

Bob Cheyne, who was Arkansas' sports information director during Broyles' glory years, said, "You wouldn't have wanted a game to be more intense than Arkansas-Texas was. Yet Frank and Darrell got along great. If every relationship between coaches would be that healthy, that would be wonderful. It wasn't as if they wouldn't do anything they could to win a ballgame, but they each admired the values of the other person."

They certainly had great games against each other. During the 1960s, the winner of the Arkansas-Texas game also won the

Frank Broyles (right) and Darrell Royal (left) coached against each other in Arkansas-Texas classics for 19 years.

Southwest Conference eight times. Arkansas and Texas trailed only Alabama in total victories among collegiate teams during that decade. Texas won two national championships and the Razorbacks won one.

Texas had dominated Arkansas for years, until Mickey Cissell's fourth quarter field goal gave the Hogs a 24–23 win at Austin in 1960. Broyles recalled, "That's the game that put us on the map. Beating Texas at Austin gave us the opportunity to recruit in Texas."

Arkansas' only conference losses in 1961 and 1962 were to Texas. In 1964, the Razorbacks defeated the Longhorns 14–13 at Austin and didn't lose a game en route to the post-bowl versions of the national championship. The Hogs won a 27–24 thriller over the 'Horns at Fayetteville in 1965. Texas was ranked No. 1 nationally going into the '64 and '65 games.

The Razorbacks made it three in a row against Texas in 1966 at Austin. In 1968, the Hogs went 10-1 and earned a victory over Georgia in the Sugar Bowl. The only defeat? Texas, of course.

While Broyles' Arkansas teams twice beat Texas when the Longhorns were ranked No. 1, the most remembered game of the Broyles-Royal rivalry was the "Big Shootout of 1969." Texas overcame a 14–0 deficit with two fourth-quarter touchdowns to nab a 15–14 win. The matchup came at the end of the season. Both teams were undefeated. Texas was ranked No. 1; Arkansas No. 2.

"The 1960s were the best decade ever for Arkansas football," Cheyne said. "Texas was the only real rival we had, and we came out in pretty good shape with them. I don't care what they say about Army-Navy, Southern Cal–Notre Dame or Alabama-Auburn. One of the greatest rivalries in college football was Arkansas-Texas during Frank and Darrell's years."

Broyles' last hurrah against Royal came in 1971, when Joe Ferguson threw all over the Longhorns in a 31–7 UA win at Little Rock. Royal's teams won the last five matchups between the two Hall of Fame coaches, including the 1976 game, which was the last for both coaches.

"I had told the University of Arkansas administration that the 1976 season would be my last," Broyles said. "We kept it quiet all season, until a day or two before playing Texas, which was our last game that year. I was visiting with Darrell on the phone in late October when he told me it was going to be his last year. I told him he couldn't quit coaching then because it was my last year. It was ironic we went out against each other."

Broyles remained at Arkansas as athletic director for another three decades. Royal stayed at Texas as a special consultant to the president. The pair made trips together and played golf frequently long after they finished their coaching careers.

Royal's death in 2013 was a jolt to Broyles. "He was a great coach and a great friend," said Broyles. "I miss him."

45 Outland Winners: Loyd Phillips and Bud Brooks

After a four-year period during which Arkansas had won a grand total of 12 games, little was expected of the Razorbacks as the 1954 season approached. Sports information director Bob Cheyne could never have anticipated the opportunities he would have to publicize several Razorbacks players during the extraordinary season that came.

One of Arkansas' best that year was lineman Bud Brooks, steady on offense but spectacular on defense. Surprisingly, for Cheyne, it was the only time in his 21-year career with the Razorbacks that he clashed with the coaching staff on spotlighting a player for national honors.

"Many of Bud Brooks' great plays on defense came from being out of position," Cheyne recalled. "The ball would go in a direction where he wasn't supposed to be, but he'd be there to make the tackle. His hole might have been open. But great football players play instinctively and he would know what the play was going to be. The players greatly admired that intellect in Bud."

Cheyne's efforts paid off. As Arkansas kept winning, eventually earning the Southwest Conference championship, Brooks gained national attention. Eventually he not only was named to nearly

Burlingame for Heisman

Before the 1979 football season began, senior Mike Burlingame, a returning starter at center, asked who the Heisman Trophy candidates were that year. When he was told that every collegiate player was eligible to win the top individual award presented to a college football player, Burlingame declared himself a candidate.

"I touch the ball on every play," Burlingame said. "No one else but the quarterback does that. I'm never offside. I play on a great team. That should help my chances, too." Burlingame did indeed play on a great team. The Razorbacks went 10–1 during the regular season and earned a spot opposite top-ranked Alabama in the Sugar Bowl. Every week, Burlingame came up with clever comments for the press, including the week he had to miss a game because of injury. "That shouldn't hurt the campaign," he said. "I will have more time for interviews."

Burlingame's head coach, Lou Holtz, himself a quipster, didn't quite know how to take the tongue-in-cheek campaign. "I don't think he minded because it helped keep the team loose," Burlingame speculated. Alas, Burlingame didn't win the coveted award, despite going to such lengths as posing for a picture in the famous Heisman pose. Instead the honors went to Charles White, a Southern Cal running back with considerably better statistics than Burlingame. But the campaign worked to some extent. He actually got a few votes, thanks to sportswriters who appreciated Burlingame's sense of humor.

every All-America team, but he also was the first Razorback ever to win the Outland Trophy, given annually to the best lineman (including linebackers) in college football.

"It was the only time I was ever accused of overpublicizing a player," Cheyne said. "But he deserved it because of his ability to challenge a play that wasn't necessarily designed to come into his area. I don't remember a single time a play went through a hole that he had deserted. He knew where they were going to run and he was there. And he was a very sure tackler."

Loyd Phillips won the Outland Trophy in 1966 and was a two-time All-American.

Bud Brooks was the Outland Trophy winner in 1954.

No one doubted Cheyne's judgment when it came to promoting Arkansas' second Outland winner, defensive tackle Loyd Phillips, who won the award in 1966. "Loyd was absolutely incredible," Cheyne said. "If you would have taken a poll among every player on our team when Loyd was a sophomore [1964], they would have said he would be the player to be honored most. He was such an incredible sophomore that I didn't know what more I could say about him after that year. It struck me early in his career that he was one of the greatest players in Arkansas football history.

"Loyd had unbelievable raw talent. He was great to work with, and never sought any of the honors he won. We lost to Texas Tech in the last game of his senior season, costing us a chance to go to the Cotton Bowl for the third consecutive year. He was disappointed and thought it was his worst game of the year. I was telling him that he would be on all the All-American teams and shared what all-star games he would be playing in. He didn't particularly like [hearing] that after a loss. He said to give the honors to the team."

Despite his aversion to honors, Phillips was a deserving winner of the Outland Trophy. In those days, the player didn't actually receive a trophy to keep. Forty years later that situation was rectified, and Phillips at last received the trophy he won as one of the greatest Razorbacks ever.

46 Thumper

Born in Hampton, Arkansas, and a high school All-American at El Dorado, Wayne Harris was the picture of greatness as a Razorbacks linebacker. In fact, Wilson Matthews, who coached Harris and several other outstanding linebackers at Arkansas, once

Wayne Harris earned the nickname "Thumper" for his ferocious hits.

said, "Wayne Harris is the finest linebacker I've ever seen. No one hit like he did."

After he blasted SMU quarterback Don Meredith and knocked him out of the game for a while, Matthews said, "It's hard to see your receiver when your eyeballs are in the back of your head."

That hard-hitting ability is the reason why they called him "Thumper." As a senior, he made a staggering 174 tackles. At the time, the Hogs only played 10 regular season games, and bowl game statistics didn't count toward a player's numbers. Even so, it has been a school record ever since—no one has come closer than Ken Hamlin, who made 159 tackles in 2002.

Harris also played center on offense, and as a senior he was named consensus All-America on both offense and defense. He also was named the Southwest Conference Player of the Year, a rare honor for a non-skill-position player.

A starter on Frank Broyles' first team that lost its initial six games before winning four in a row, Harris anchored Arkansas' Southwest Conference champions of 1959 and 1960, which played in the Gator and Cotton Bowl games, respectively.

Broyles noted, "Wayne wasn't very big. He weighed 182 pounds when he played for us—but he would hit you. As an offensive lineman, he was a great blocker. He hit as hard when he was blocking as he did when he made a tackle. He became one of the greatest players ever in the Canadian Football League."

Harris was All-CFL in nine of his 12 seasons with the Calgary Stampeders. He made 28 career interceptions, and was the Most Valuable Player of the Grey Cup (the CFL's championship game) in 1971 when he helped Calgary become the only team in CFL history to go undefeated.

Also an academic All-American, Harris has been inducted into the CFL, College Football, Arkansas, and University of Arkansas Halls of Fame.

47 Bill McClard

Even though he grew up in Norman, Oklahoma, at a time when the Sooners were a football powerhouse, and even though he was the most highly recruited kicker in the country as a high school senior, Bill McClard chose Arkansas when head coach Frank Broyles promised him he would break all of the school's kicking records.

"Coach Broyles was in my home eight times, and Jim Lindsey, who had played at Arkansas and was with the Minnesota Vikings at the time, came to Norman every Thursday to take me to lunch," said McClard. "Arkansas' facilities at the time weren't very good. They didn't compare to Oklahoma or Texas. But [Oklahoma's] Chuck Fairbanks told me they had signed a kicker and I would have to redshirt. Texas had a kicker.

"Coach Broyles told me there would be a lot of opportunities for a kicker to score points with the team he was putting together. He was right. By the time I was through, I had the NCAA record for points by a kicker, and for extra points."

McClard's UA career PAT record stood for nearly 40 years—and that was just three seasons' worth, since freshmen weren't eligible to play varsity football at the time. He also was the first Razorbacks kicker to score more than 200 points (212) during his career.

He also was the first collegiate ever to kick a 60-yard field goal. He did it against SMU at Fayetteville in 1970. "It was an ideal day for field goals," McClard recalled. "The wind was blowing out of the north at 10 to 15 miles per hour. In warm-ups I hit six field goals from 68 yards on eight tries."

Near the end of the first half, Arkansas had the wind to its back and Broyles elected to let McClard try a 60-yarder. The NCAA record at the time was 57 yards. The wind helped; McClard's kick was low, but it hit the crossbar and went through. The stadium rocked with energy. No one had ever seen a 60-yard field goal before.

McClard kicked for teams that had a cumulative record of 26–7–1. Afterward, he spent several years in the NFL. And perhaps those early lunches with Lindsey paid off—McClard later went to work for Lindsey Real Estate in northwest Arkansas.

Steve Little

Lon Farrell, an assistant coach turned administrator, loved to tell the story of recruiting Steve Little. In today's world of recruitment mania, Little would have been a five-star recruit. Even in the 1970s, he was pursued by numerous schools, some of which made illegal offers.

"I told him that whatever money he was being offered wouldn't last long, and eventually a car turns to rust. But being a Razorback is something that will last forever," Farrell said.

It must have convinced the Shawnee Mission, Kansas, native. A superb quarterback in high school, Little become arguably the greatest in a line of great kickers at Arkansas.

Many of Little's records have since been broken, but the Hogs have never had a greater weapon in the kicking game. Nearly all of his kickoffs (then from the 40-yard line) sailed out of the end zone. He kicked more long field goals, including an NCAA record 67-yarder against Texas, than any Razorback. And he was a terrific punter, too.

Though he clearly had unimpeachable talent at his position, Little pleaded with head coach Frank Broyles for a chance to play quarterback. "Steve was too valuable as a kicker to use at quarterback," Broyles said. "If he hadn't been such a good kicker, he could have been an outstanding quarterback. He was an exceptional athlete."

Little's peak year was 1977, his only season under the direction of head coach Lou Holtz. He kicked 19 field goals and averaged 44.3 yards per punt on 48 kicks. His career average of 44.4 yards per punt is still tied for second in school history.

He remains the only Razorback with two field goals of longer than 60 yards. One of them, a 67-yarder, was among three field goals he kicked against Texas in a 13–9 loss in 1977. He also had a 61-yarder against Tulsa during his junior campaign.

Little added seven long field goals between 50 and 59 yards, giving him nine three-pointers of more than 50 yards. By comparison, no other UA kicker has produced more than four field goals of 50 yards or more.

In Little's last game, his kickoffs and third-quarter field goal gave Arkansas a major boost in its 31–6 victory against second-ranked Oklahoma in the 1978 Orange Bowl. "Oklahoma decided to take the ball to start the game," recalled Hogs quarterback Ron Calcagni. "As usual, Steve kicked it into the end zone. In fact, he kicked it into the stands. That gave us great field position. Oklahoma fumbled on the third play of the game. We recovered and scored a quick touchdown. Steve's kicks gave us good field position all night."

Little was such a weapon he was drafted in the first round by the St. Louis (now Arizona) Cardinals. At Arkansas, he was able to use a tee for all his kicks, including field goals. But the NFL did not allow tees for field goals and extra points. Little didn't adapt well, and was cut during his second season. Later paralyzed in an automobile accident, he never had another opportunity to utilize his incredible ability.

49 Paul Eells

"Oh my!" escaped from Paul Eells' lips more times than anyone could count during his tenure as "Voice of the Razorbacks." Eells had the most familiar voice in Arkansas, and a style that made everyone who listened to him believe he was one of his or her best friends. When you heard his voice, you knew the Razorbacks were on.

"That's exactly what we were looking for," said Frank Broyles, the UA athletic director who worked with Dale Nicholson, long-time general manager at KATV, to hire a voice for the Hogs and sports director for Little Rock's ABC affiliate. "We always wanted someone whose voice was that of a friend to Razorback fans. Paul was that. When his voice came through the radio, it was as if he was talking directly to each listener."

Eells was working for a TV station in Nashville and calling Vanderbilt games when he interviewed with Nicholson and Broyles. After visiting with Nicholson he flew to Fayetteville, where he met Broyles on the golf course. "I thought the time with Coach Broyles went well," Eells said shortly before his death in 2006. "We had finished talking and just before he teed off he said, 'I'll see you soon.' At that point I thought I had the job."

Amazing as it seems, Arkansas' first game of the 1978 football season, Eells' initial season as the team's voice, was against Vanderbilt. The schools hadn't played in years and were in different conferences—Arkansas in the Southwest Conference and Vandy in the Southeastern Conference. "It was really strange," Eells said at the time. "I actually knew the Vanderbilt players better than I knew the players for the Razorbacks."

It didn't take Eells long to become familiar with the Hogs—or to become that friendly voice Broyles desired for Razorbacks fans. Eells broadcast football and basketball for several years before the increased number of in-state telecasts required him to do football only on the radio so he could handle play-by-play of the basketball telecasts.

Mike Nail worked with Eells on the football broadcasts for several years and eventually replaced Eells as radio play-by-play man for basketball. Nail said, "Paul was a great broadcaster and outstanding person. I never heard him say a bad word about anyone. Paul was very much in love with his job. He loved being the voice of Razorback football. He was always well prepared and did a great job of describing the action."

Eells had a number of famous calls, including U.S. Reed's half-court buzzer beater that lifted Arkansas past defending national champion Louisville in the 1981 NCAA Tournament, DeCori Birmingham's "Miracle on Markham" catch against LSU in 2002, Clint Stoerner's touchdown pass to Anthony Lucas to defeat Tennessee in 1999, and Todd Wright's field goal that gave the Hogs a victory over the Vols at Knoxville in 1992.

Victories over Tennessee were especially satisfying to Eells since he rarely saw the Vols vanquished while at Vandy. "If Arkansas beats Tennessee today, I'll go down on the field and run a lap around the stadium," Eells said before the 1992 football game at Knoxville in Arkansas' first year in the SEC. As much as he wanted to, Eells didn't actually run that victory lap.

Eells was still going strong with KATV and the Razorbacks and was preparing for his 29th season as "Voice of the Razorbacks" when tragedy occurred. Eells played in Houston Nutt's preseason golf tournament just before preseason practice began in 2006 when he died in a car accident on the way home. The entire state of Arkansas was stunned.

He never considered himself as a celebrity, and he treated everyone—from the head coach to a student assistant who would hand him a flip card—as if he or she was the most important person in the world. That's why the state mourned when it lost Paul Eells as the "Voice of the Razorbacks."

50 Bud Campbell

Bud Campbell was sports director at KATV in Little Rock when University of Arkansas athletic director John Barnhill decided it would be best for the school's expansive radio network to have a voice from central Arkansas describing Razorbacks football games.

At the time, Bob Cheyne was not only the sports information director but also did radio play-by-play for Razorbacks football and basketball. He had been doing it for nearly a decade when Barnhill decided to make the change.

"I could tell when Barney called me into his office one day shortly before the football season that something was up," said Cheyne. "He said the department had made a decision for Bud Campbell to do football. It hurt me, but I could see it was the best decision for the athletic department. It was important to have someone from central Arkansas doing the games."

Campbell's voice became legendary. He called some of Arkansas' greatest games, including the Big Shootout with Texas in 1969. He also called some regional games for ABC, since his station in Little Rock was the largest ABC affiliate in the state.

"Bud was a friend and did a great job announcing our games and working with me on our TV show," said Frank Broyles, whose program was among the nation's best during Campbell's time.

It was a great era for sports radio, and one of Arkansas' affiliates was 50,000-watt KAAY, a Little Rock powerhouse whose night-time signal could be heard in every surrounding state and then some. Campbell's voice delivered information on UA games to Razorbacks fans far beyond the state's borders.

Voice of the Razorbacks and sports director at KATV, Little Rock, Bud Campbell interviews UA quarterback Bill Montgomery.

Campbell's tenure, like Eells' would years later, ended suddenly. During the 1974 season he was killed in a car accident while driving home one night. The state was shocked.

"It was a tragic loss," Broyles said. "He had good relations with many of the major broadcasters of that time. Chris Schenkel, who was the lead voice on ABC football during the early 1970s, came to Little Rock to host my TV show that Sunday out of the respect he had for Bud."

51 Bobby Petrino

With Frank Broyles retiring as athletic director and head football coach Houston Nutt resigning after 10 years with the Razorbacks, the first task awaiting new athletic director Jeff Long was to hire a football coach after the 2007 season.

"We needed someone tough enough to compete in the SEC," said Long. "This isn't a conference for the meek and mild. We needed someone who was a sitting head coach and had succeeded at a high level. Knowing it would be difficult to attract someone like that, I knew I had to be aggressive in recruiting.

"I had known Bobby Petrino when I was athletic director at Pittsburgh and he was head football coach at Louisville. I had seen his teams, how good they were and how talented they were. I knew his reputation as a strategic mind. When it became known to me he would have an interest, I became interested."

Petrino had left Louisville for the glamour of pro football but was suffering through a difficult first year with the Atlanta Falcons. Behind the scenes he let it be known he would welcome an opportunity to return to college coaching, especially in the SEC.

"Everything played out," Long said. "He left the Falcons before their season was over to take our job. That was a choice he had to make because I wasn't in a position to wait. He made a very difficult decision, one we benefitted from, when he became our head coach."

Petrino's first team was 5–7, but beat LSU in the season finale with a last-second touchdown. His second squad was 8–5 and won the Liberty Bowl. But Petrino's first two seasons were mere scene-setters for what was to come.

In 2010 with Ryan Mallett—a transfer from Michigan in his second year as starting quarterback—and loaded with great receivers, Arkansas won 10 regular-season games for only the second time since entering the SEC in 1992. A season-ending victory over LSU landed the Razorbacks a spot in the Sugar Bowl. It was the first time since the system began in the late 1990s that Arkansas played in a BCS bowl.

Long said, "That was an exciting time for us. It was proof that we could do it at Arkansas. Our fans came and supported us. It was a great atmosphere. History will look back on the problems Ohio State had and whether some of their players [investigated by the NCAA] should have played or not, but the truth is, we wanted to beat them at full strength. A scoop and score on a blocked punt and we would have won the Sugar Bowl."

Unfortunately, the Hogs fell on the loose ball after blocking the punt and threw an interception in the final seconds to fall short by five points.

In 2011, Mallett was gone, but Tyler Wilson took the reins at quarterback—and the Hogs were explosive again. They repeated their 10 regular-season wins, then defeated Kansas State in the Cotton Bowl. Arkansas was 11–2 and ranked fifth in the final polls. It was the best finish since the 1977 Hogs went 11–1 and finished third nationally.

"Coach Petrino set a high standard," said Mallett. "With him you always knew what you were supposed to do and how you were supposed to do it. When we got back to school after the Liberty Bowl, we started off-season workouts at five in the morning. We actually liked it. He instilled that in us. He made me a better quarterback."

Tim Horton, an assistant coach on Petrino's staff, added, "Coach Petrino is an excellent X's and O's coach. His attention to detail and the way he demanded execution was as good as there has ever been. He is very driven, and drives the team hard. He is very smart. He has a plan for everything. Much like Lou Holtz and Ken Hatfield, he has a great offensive mind."

Alas, Petrino's tenure ended suddenly in the April after the Cotton Bowl victory, when an off-the-field incident forced his termination. Long's decision was necessary, but years later Long said, "Bobby remains one of the most intelligent football coaches I've known."

52 First BCS Bowl

If there had been a Bowl Championship Series in the 1960s, Arkansas would have played in major bowl games six times. As it was, the Hogs made four trips to the Sugar Bowl during that decade. The Razorbacks returned to the Sugar Bowl following the 1979 season but hadn't been back since when they were invited to play in the contest following the 2010 season.

The Bowl Championship Series was started in 1998 as a better way to determine the national champion. Four bowls, the Orange, Sugar, Fiesta, and Rose, were involved, along with a national title game that rotated among those four sites. The Hogs had been to plenty of bowl games between '98 and 2010, but never to a BCS bowl.

The opponent was Ohio State, and it was a great opportunity for the Razorbacks to face one of the nation's top programs. The Buckeyes came into the contest swirling in controversy. Five of their players were under investigation by the NCAA. In the end, all were allowed to play, then were suspended for several games the following season.

For its part, Arkansas had enjoyed a spectacular 10–2 season, losing only to Alabama when the Crimson Tide was ranked No. 1, and to Auburn, the eventual national champion. Led by quarterback Ryan Mallett, who passed for more than 3,000 yards, running back Knile Davis, who rushed for over 1,000 and a bevy of quality wide receivers, the Razorbacks faced LSU in the season finale with the Sugar Bowl on the line.

"We had gone 8–5 the year before, but inside our locker room we thought we had a legitimate shot at the national championship," said Mallett. "Not many people gave us a chance but if you change two plays from that season, we would be playing for the national title.

"We wanted to set a standard for future Arkansas teams to play at a high level. We didn't win the national championship, but we accomplished our goal when we beat LSU and became the first Razorback team to play in a BCS bowl."

Athletic director Jeff Long added, "It was a great experience for our fans. It was close enough to Arkansas for our fans to show up in large numbers. Their support was amazing."

Tim Horton, former Razorbacks wide receiver and an assistant coach on Bobby Petrino's staff said, "I had lived Razorback history my entire life, and the setting reminded me of Reunion Arena in Dallas, when we used to dominate the crowd at the Southwest Conference basketball tournament. At least 70 percent of the crowd had to be Razorback fans. It was a lot like times we would play in the Cotton Bowl. I loved the great pride Arkansas fans showed in finally winning big enough to make that first BCS trip. It was a great game. We played well and should have won."

Despite a 17-yard touchdown pass from Mallett to Joe Adams that temporarily tied the game at seven all in the first quarter, the Hogs fell behind 28–7 before Zach Hocker kicked a field goal to close the first half.

The teams traded field goals early in the third quarter. Ohio State led 31–13 when the Razorbacks launched a comeback. Mallett hit Jarius Wright for a 22-yard touchdown, then found D.J. Williams for the two-point conversion.

Early in the fourth quarter, Jake Bequette tackled Ohio State's Dan Herron in the end zone for a safety. After the Buckeyes kicked to the Hogs, Arkansas marched close enough for Hocker to kick a 47-yard field goal that made it 31–26.

The Hogs couldn't do much after that, until late in the game, Ohio State punted with a little more than a minute left. Colton Miles-Nash blocked it for the Hogs. Julian Horton had a clear shot at a scoop-and-score touchdown, but he fell on the ball at the Ohio State 18.

"We always tell our players to secure the ball first," said Petrino after the game.

There was still 1:09 left on the clock—plenty of time for the winning touchdown. But on second down the Buckeyes dropped an end into coverage and Mallett threw an interception that quashed Arkansas' chances.

"We were proud to be the first Razorback team to play in a BCS bowl, but we all wish we had won the game," Mallett said.

Jarius Wright

Jarius Wright is the only Razorback receiver ever to catch touchdown passes in three different bowl games. He didn't know that until he was interviewed for this book. "I would never have known if you hadn't told me," Wright said. "I never really paid attention to records. I just played and tried to win games. Fortunately, we won two of those bowl games and almost won the other."

A freshman during Bobby Petrino's first year as coach, Wright didn't go to a bowl game during the 5–7 season. So when the Razorbacks met East Carolina in the 2010 Liberty Bowl, Wright

Jarius Wright catches a touchdown pass in the 2011 Sugar Bowl. (AP Images)

considered it the biggest game of his career. "It was my biggest game because we didn't go to a bowl when I was a freshman, and a bowl game is where you want to be," Wright said. "So up to that point, it was my biggest game."

Obviously the Sugar and Cotton Bowl games of the next two years were even bigger, but they may never be as memorable as the Liberty Bowl was because of the conditions. "It was cold all week and Bobby took it easy on us at practice," Wright recalled. "It was freezing cold the day of the game. We got to the stadium and the wind was swirling. I remember in pregame how hard it was to catch punts and passes."

With icy temperatures in Memphis and a quarterback, Ryan Mallett, who threw lasers, how did Wright manage to catch the ball at all? "I just had to ignore how cold it was," Wright answered. "It was a big game."

Wright's hands stayed warm long enough to make four catches for 90 yards, including a 41-yard touchdown grab to tie the game in the fourth quarter. "We ran one of Bobby's favorite plays," Wright said. "I scored a lot of touchdowns on it during my career, including against Kansas State in the Cotton Bowl two years later. Mallett threw a great pass. The safety misjudged it and it fell right into my hands.

"Even after the touchdown I didn't know if we would win the game. East Carolina missed three field goals, then we kicked one in overtime to win. We all felt a lot better after winning."

A year later, Arkansas was 10–2 and earned a spot opposite Ohio State in the Sugar Bowl. It was the first BCS experience for the Razorbacks.

Ohio State led 31-13 in the fourth quarter when, Wright said, "Mallett called a hitch route. If the defensive back presses, I run a go route. I was licking my chops. It was a mismatch for me. Mallett put the ball right in my hands. I knew I had to make a play."

Unaware of His Records

Can you imagine setting several school records and never knowing it? That was the case with Razorbacks wide receiver Jarius Wright. The Warren native, who played four years for Coach Bobby Petrino, had to be told about the numbers he was amassing.

"Reporters would ask me how I felt about the records I was approaching or had broken," Wright said. "I wouldn't know what they were talking about. Before I came to Arkansas I never dreamed I would set records. I just wanted to play and win football games."

Wright's superlatives? He set records for catches (66) and receiving yards (1,117) in a season (since broken by Cobi Hamilton). He had 168 career catches (also a record until Hamilton passed him) and earned 2,934 yards (which Hamilton didn't pass). His 12 touchdown catches in a season is still a record. Those are pretty good numbers for a guy who wasn't aware of them. And, he's still catching passes—now for Minnesota in the NFL.

He did—it was a 22-yard touchdown. The Hogs added a two-point conversion and rallied in the fourth quarter before falling 31-26.

Things were better the following year in the Cotton Bowl. Arkansas dominated Kansas State for its 11th win of the year. Wright had three catches for 88 yards, including another touchdown.

"It was the same route: down the middle," Wright said. "Tyler Wilson threw this one. It was great to play a part in winning 11 games. We made it as high as No. 3 in the rankings before we played LSU and we finished No. 5."

Incidentally, the TD he scored against Kansas State was similar to a TD catch he made against Texas A&M earlier that year, in the same stadium, when he tied the UA record for most receptions in a game with 13.

After his sensational 2011 season, he was drafted by the Minnesota Vikings, where he has become a solid wideout.

"I really think his work ethic made Jarius a professional player," said Tim Horton, an assistant coach at Arkansas for Wright's entire career. "He was good in high school, but went to a new level in college. He was as good as anyone I've ever been around at pushing off the line. Just like that fast car that can go from zero to 60 in two seconds, Jarius got on the defensive back in a hurry."

So, although he is still catching footballs in the NFL, Wright will always be remembered for his brilliant career as a Razorback. And now he knows he is the only Razorback ever to catch touchdown passes in three different bowl games.

54 Tyler Wilson

When you look at the best single-season passing efforts at the University of Arkansas, two names stand out. They are Ryan Mallett and Tyler Wilson. Mallett had the first and third highest totals ever. Wilson was second and fourth. But at the top of the career passing yards list is Wilson, who almost wasn't a Razorback.

When Wilson was a senior at Greenwood High School, Houston Nutt was Arkansas' head coach. For whatever reason, Nutt never offered Wilson a scholarship. Wilson was prepared to go to Tulsa, where he had committed, when Bobby Petrino became the Razorbacks coach. Tim Horton, who was Nutt's recruiting coordinator, and who remained at Arkansas to work with Petrino, convinced the new coach to look at Wilson.

"We thought Tyler would do well in Coach Petrino's offense," said Horton. "Rick Jones at Greenwood runs a sophisticated passing offense, and that gave Tyler a chance to thrive under Coach Petrino."

Wilson's first year was fairly uneventful. He played in two games, throwing a touchdown pass against Alabama, before being sidelined with an illness that allowed him to receive a medical hardship waiver. Upon recuperation, his return was completely overshadowed by the arrival of Ryan Mallett, who had transferred from Michigan and became eligible in 2009.

"I learned a lot from Ryan," Wilson said at the time. "I knew how good he was and that it would be difficult to be a starter. I knew I would have to wait for my time."

Wilson played well when opportunities came, especially when Mallett was injured early in the 2010 Auburn game. Competing against the team that would eventually win the national title, Wilson completed 25 of his 34 passes for 332 yards and four touchdowns. The Hogs didn't win, but it was a coming-out party for Wilson.

Mallett was still the starter, and returned the following week, but Petrino noted at the time, "Tyler did a good job under pressure. He was prepared to play when we needed him."

Mallett finished spectacularly and led the Razorbacks to a berth in the Sugar Bowl. He then declared for the NFL Draft, and the job went to Wilson. He took full advantage.

In his fifth start, Wilson had a game unlike any Razorbacks quarterback ever has experienced. Arkansas trailed Texas A&M at halftime at the Dallas Cowboys' stadium, and Wilson came out firing. When the day was over, the Razorbacks earned a 42–38 triumph as Wilson completed 30 of his 51 passes for 510 yards and three touchdowns. He broke Mallett's single-game passing yardage record by more than 100 yards.

Jarius Wright was on the receiving end of 13 of Wilson's passes that day, tying Wear Schoonover's record from 1929. Wright scored two of the touchdowns and amassed 281 receiving yards, a record until broken by Cobi Hamilton a year later.

"Tyler threw the ball hard," Wright said. "He didn't throw as hard as Mallett, but hardly anyone does. We could run anything

Cobi Sets a Record

After playing for teams that earned spots in the Sugar and Cotton Bowl games and won 21 games during a two-year period, wide receiver Cobi Hamilton was poised for a great senior season. After all, quarterback Tyler Wilson had turned down an opportunity to enter the NFL Draft to return for his senior season. But things started going sour in the spring when the Hogs lost head coach Petrino. John L. Smith was named the interim coach. Wilson, Hamilton, and the other seniors would have to be the leaders.

It wasn't easy, especially after the Hogs started 1–2. Facing Rutgers at Reynolds Razorback Stadium, Arkansas tried to turn things around. "I remember the game vividly," said Tim Horton, an assistant coach at the time. "We lost because we had a hard time stopping them. But Cobi and Tyler displayed a will to win that showed as much determination as I've ever seen. They were animated. They were trying to get us over the hump."

Wilson passed for 419 yards that day and Hamilton became the first Razorback to earn more than 300 receiving yards in a game when he made 10 catches for 303 yards and three touchdowns. His scores covered 57, 10, and 80 yards. "A whole bunch of those 303 yards came after the catch," said Horton. "There were a lot of crossing patterns, where he would catch the ball then run anywhere from 20 to 60 yards."

Things didn't get much better for the Razorbacks, who won only three more games that year. But Hamilton never slowed down. He caught 90 passes during the campaign to shatter Jarius Wright's UA record 66. He also broke Wright's receiving yardage record with 1,335 yards. It may be a while before anyone approaches Hamilton's records, especially his single-game superlative.

with Tyler that we had run with Ryan. I was a senior when Tyler was a junior. We had a lot of great receivers that year. With Tyler at quarterback, we had a great offense."

The offense was prolific enough to thrust Arkansas into the No. 3 spot in the national polls going into the regular-season finale against LSU. The Razorbacks didn't win, but were invited to the Cotton Bowl, where they defeated Kansas State.

Wilson started every game of that 2011 season. He passed for 3,638 yards, second only to Mallett's best season. More importantly, Arkansas won 11 games for only the third time in its history. The first time, 1964, Freddy Marshall was the quarterback for the most part; he missed the first two games of the year and Bill Gray started. Ron Calcagni started every game in 1977. Thus, Wilson and Calcagni are the only quarterbacks ever to direct the Razorbacks to 11 victories in a single season.

Wilson could have left for the NFL Draft after the 2011 season, but after talking to Petrino he decided to return for 2012.

"Growing up in Arkansas, it was an honor to be the Razorback quarterback," Wilson said at the time. "We had the potential to be very good again and I wanted to be part of it."

After it was too late for Wilson to reconsider his decision, Petrino was dismissed and John L. Smith became interim head coach. Optimism disappeared early in the season, when the Hogs lost to Louisiana-Monroe in the second game. Wilson was injured in the first half of the matchup and did not return. The Razorbacks lost in overtime.

Arkansas won only four games that season, but it wasn't Wilson's fault. He took a physical pounding at times but played nearly every minute on offense after the Louisiana-Monroe game. He passed for 3,387 yards. That's the fourth highest total in school history, behind two of Mallett's seasons and one of his own.

Wilson finished his career with a school record 7,765 yards— 272 more than Mallett. Today, with Bret Bielema as coach, even though his offense is balanced with plenty of throwing, it is doubtful if any quarterback will approach Wilson's numbers any time in the near future. Even though his last season wasn't what he hoped for, Wilson will always be remembered by Razorbacks fans as the quarterback who stayed when he could have left early.

55 Mike Anderson Returns

An assistant coach at Arkansas for 17 glorious years, Mike Anderson was a fan favorite head coaching prospect after John Pelphrey was dismissed. However, just because Anderson had spent so many years in Fayetteville as Nolan Richardson's assistant didn't mean he would return.

Anderson was completing his fifth season of coaching at Missouri. He had taken the Tigers to three straight NCAA Tournaments and believed his sixth team would be his best. He had done a magnificent job at Alabama-Birmingham in his first head coaching position, which he took after being passed on for the head coaching job at Arkansas after its winningest coach, Nolan Richardson, was dismissed.

"When Arkansas became available and I visited with [athletic director] Jeff Long, I had to make one of the most difficult decisions I've ever had to make," said Anderson. "Leaving Missouri wasn't in our plans. We had seven seniors returning, a good young nucleus and commitments from some other outstanding recruits. We had created a culture. There was a lot of energy in the program."

While Anderson wrestled with the decision, Long hoped Anderson would say yes—not because he had been at Arkansas but because of his record at Alabama-Birmingham and Missouri. "I had interest in Mike Anderson because I saw what he did at UAB and Missouri, to build programs at those schools," Long said. "I didn't know Mike Anderson the assistant for Nolan Richardson. But I knew the condition of Missouri's program when he got there and I saw what he built there.

"Mike had always impressed me with his success in turning programs. You look at his academic record at both places: it was outstanding. You look for discipline and accountability in his program: it was outstanding. You look for a coach who you want to win games and championships, but ultimately you are trying to develop young people into being the best people they can be and go on to be successful in life. Mike Anderson gets that."

Long had never met Anderson before interviewing him for the job. He knew Anderson has been there with Richardson, but was impressed because "Mike was his own man, his own coach and had achieved a level of success. Having all that Arkansas history was a bonus. He knew the fabric of the program, what it should be, what it can be, the heights it can reach. Once I sat down with him, it was an easy decision to try to hire Mike Anderson as our head basketball coach."

Anderson said he "prayed a lot and sought counsel from my closest friends. Once we decided to make the change, it was exciting. I'm pleased to be at Arkansas. The blessing has been, we've always left a program in better shape than we found it."

Anderson found Arkansas' program in a difficult academic situation. He won 18 and 19 games in his first two seasons, while building a foundation for year three. His third team made it to the National Invitation Tournament, Arkansas' first postseason appearance in six years.

He also made it difficult for opponents to win at Bud Walton Arena again. His first three Razorback teams were 51–6 at Bud Walton. The Hogs beat Kentucky twice and every other SEC team at least once at Bud Walton during that time. It was obvious the program was on the upswing.

"The foundation has been built," Anderson said. "We expect to get better and better and always been in a position to play in the NCAA Tournament."

56 U.S. Reed Beats Louisville

Scotty Thurman hit a three-point shot with the 35-second clock approaching zero to snap a tie and lead Arkansas to a national championship game victory over Duke in 1994. But before that unforgettable buzzer-beater, there was no doubt in the minds of Arkansas fans about what was the most famous shot in Razorbacks history. And that half-court shot made by U.S. Reed still gains attention more than 30 years later.

Louisville was the defending national champion when the Cardinals and Razorbacks met in the second round of the 1981 NCAA tournament. As it happened, the Razorbacks had been the last team to beat Louisville in NCAA Tournament play; Sidney Moncrief and the Hogs eliminated the Cardinals in the 1979 tourney.

It looked like the Razorbacks were about to knock Louisville out again in 1981, leading for nearly the entire game. But the Cardinals hit two free throws with five seconds left to take a 73–72 lead. UA coach Eddie Sutton called timeout.

"Just like he always did, Coach Sutton told us someone was going to win this game," Reed recalled. "He would usually look at whoever he wanted to take the last shot while he was saying that. He told me to get as close as I could and shoot it, or if I couldn't get a shot off to try to pass it to Scott Hastings or someone closer to the basket. There were only five seconds left, so I didn't know if there would be time for that. I figured I would get as close as I could, then shoot it.

"It's funny, but before that game, in the warm-ups, I was shooting the ball from farther away than I normally did. I was way outside. Some of the guys were asking me why I was doing that. I

U.S. Reed (left) and Darrell Walker celebrate the victory against the defending national champions, which Reed clinched with a buzzer-beater. (AP Images)

told them I may have to hit a long shot to win the game. I wasn't trying any shots from half court, but I was shooting longer than normal.

"One thing that did for me, it put it into my mind that if I had to take a shot like that I would have to give it a little more push than normal."

Reed took the inbounds pass, dribbled nearly to midcourt, then let it fly.

"When you let it go you know if it feels good," Reed said. "When I let it go, it felt good. After I released the ball, everything slowed down like it was in slow motion. When the ball went through the basket, everything sped up again. It was like being in the Twilight Zone."

Razorbacks players were overjoyed and the celebration commenced. Louisville players were devastated.

"I knew everyone would try to mob me so I went down press row and shook everybody's hand," Reed said. "Then I ran to the dressing room so I wouldn't get piled upon. We were in the dressing room when Abe Lemons, the Texas coach, came in wearing a Hog hat and calling the Hogs. For a moment he must have forgotten he was from Texas."

The game was played in Austin where, for the most part, the Hogs were treated rudely because of their rivalry with the Longhorns. But even the most ardent Texas fans had to admire Reed's shot. To this day U.S. hears comments about his shot.

"A friend of mine who was watching on TV when I hit the shot came up to me later and reminded me he used to watch me when I was younger and was practicing by myself in the UA–Pine Bluff Gym," said Reed. "He said I would count down from five to one, then fling a shot from half court as if it would win the game. He said, 'I used to watch you practice that.'

"One guy told me his father was a quiet man, but he'd never seen him so excited as when I hit that shot. He said it was a

Notable Dunkers

Arkansas has had plenty of basketball players who could dunk spectacularly. U.S. Reed, who at 6'2" had a 40-inch vertical, comes to mind. So does Tony Brown, who at 6'6" could ascend to nearly the top of the backboard before demonstrating a thunder dunk. And there's Sidney Moncrief, whose elevation to a dunk against Texas was magnificently captured for a 1978 *Sports Illustrated* cover. But, no Razorback's dunks have ever gone so viral as Michael Qualls'. During his sophomore year, eight of his dunks were selected among the "Top 10 Plays of the Day" for ESPN's *SportsCenter*. They were all spectacular, but none was as meaningful as the shot that beat Kentucky.

The Razorbacks and Wildcats were tied in overtime when Ky Madden launched a shot with less than five seconds remaining. Everyone, including Kentucky's players, was standing still, watching to see if it would go in, figuring it was the last attempt to prevent a second overtime. Everyone, that is, except Qualls. Madden's shot, taken from the right side, hit the rim and was bounding to the left side when Qualls timed his leap perfectly and exploded for a rebound dunk with 0.2 seconds left on the clock. The crowd at Bud Walton Arena erupted. Too late to attempt anything but desperation, the stunned Wildcats tried a length-of-the-floor pass but it caught in the netting beneath the scoreboard, where it remained for the rest of the season.

Qualls' dunk? Yes, it made *SportsCenter* and more. YouTube received thousands of views from fans who wanted to see it again and again.

bonding moment for him and his dad. Another guy told me he was so excited he jumped out of his chair and hit his head on a light fixture. He had to go to the hospital.

"A lady told me she had just had a baby and they took it to the viewing room. She heard people cheering and thought it was for her baby, but it turned out it was for the shot."

Every March, that historic shot becomes a hot topic again. "Every year, various media outlets call me and want to talk about it," Reed said. U.S. Reed and March Madness will forever be linked.

Barnhill Arena

Although Glen Rose had some excellent seasons during his two tenures as Razorbacks head basketball coach, there was no mistaking the University of Arkansas for a basketball power when John Barnhill raised enough money to build a new facility for the Razorbacks program.

"Barney could raise money," said Bob Cheyne, sports information director at the time. "We desperately needed something new for basketball. We had been playing in the old men's gym."

When Barnhill Fieldhouse opened in time for the 1957–58 season, it must have looked like a palace to Razorbacks players. Perhaps galvanized by the change in atmosphere, the Hogs actually won the Southwest Conference championship and played in the NCAA Tournament for the first time since reaching the Final Four more than two decades earlier.

"It's not much to look at today, but it was nice for its time," Cheyne said years later. "The first night we played there the scoreboard came down and splattered all over the court. John Barnhill didn't aspire to have the field house named after him, but the athletic council voted to do it."

After the 1958 season Arkansas went through another NCAA drought until Eddie Sutton was hired before the 1974–75 campaign to revive the program.

"We had to promise to renovate the building to get him to come," said Frank Broyles, then athletic director. "We did the renovation in two stages and turned it into a wonderful facility."

Before Sutton's third season, the seating capacity was raised from 5,000 to 6,200. Everything in the building, with the exception of the bleacher seats on the north side, looked brand new.

Season ticket sales skyrocketed; every game was sold out before the season began.

Arkansas won two SWC titles and advanced to the Final Four in 1978 before the second expansion was completed. Just in time for the 1978–79 season, Barnhill's capacity was raised to 9,000, and the transition from field house to arena was complete.

First under Sutton, then with Nolan Richardson as coach, Arkansas rose to national prominence—and Barnhill Arena became one of the toughest home-court advantages in college basketball. Sutton's teams were 121–8 in Barnhill. That's an astonishing percentage of .938.

Richardson's first year was a struggle (4–7 in at home) but his last seven teams that played in Barnhill were 74–8 (.902) on their

Barnhill South

Reunion Arena in Dallas was a home away from home for Razorbacks basketball fans. The Southwest Conference Tournament was played there every year but one from 1982 to 1991, Arkansas' final year in the SWC. The arena, also home of the Dallas Mavericks at the time, seated nearly 15,000. And Arkansas fans annually bought about 12,000 tickets, which indeed made it feel like a home court.

Little wonder, then, that the Razorbacks won SWC Tourney titles in Reunion in 1982, 1989, 1990, and 1991. Nolan Richardson's teams absolutely blitzed through the opposition in Arkansas' last nine SWC Tournament games, winning three consecutive titles. The closest game during that run wasn't so close: a 10-point win over Texas A&M. In the Hogs' final postseason at Reunion, they beat Texas A&M, Rice, and Texas by a combined 107 points, including a 31-point blowout in the final. Arkansas also earned its ticket to the 1990 Final Four by beating North Carolina and Texas in "Barnhill South."

Lee Mayberry, part of the 1989-91 teams said, "We always loved playing in the SWC Tournament and seeing the sea of red. As we bused to the arena we would see red everywhere. It was one of my most memorable times."

home court. No wonder Richardson was reluctant to move into a new arena, even one as spectacular as Bud Walton.

"Playing in Barnhill Arena was exciting," said Scotty Thurman, whose freshman season was Arkansas' last in the building. "It was smaller, but one of the loudest places I've ever been. We played Kentucky there in 1993 [the Hogs beat the second-ranked Wildcats] and I couldn't believe how loud it got. Barnhill was always crowded. I'm sure there were a few fire codes broken. When the game started it was packed no matter who we played."

There were many special nights in Barnhill but none more so than the last one, when Rose, Sutton, and Lanny Van Eman—all the living former Razorbacks basketball coaches—joined Richardson and his team for a celebration after the Hogs beat LSU.

Richardson, who had lost his daughter, Yvonne, to leukemia during his second season at Fayetteville, asked the fans, "Let's call the Hogs one more time for Yvonne." Jim Robken, the band director who used to race around the arena during timeouts imploring fans to get on their feet, returned and imparted the "Spirit of Barnhill" into a crystal bowl that was placed in the lobby at Bud Walton.

Even LSU coach Dale Brown, whose team had lost on its only two SEC visits to Barnhill, asked to address the gathering. Brown said, "I've been doing this for a long, long time and the fans here at Arkansas are the classiest I've ever seen."

From field house to arena, Barnhill became a phenomenal home for the Razorbacks. Still used for offices, gymnastics, and volleyball events, Barnhill lives on as a testimony to Razorbacks excellence.

58 Bud Walton Arena

Bud Walton, brother and cofounder of Walmart with Sam Walton, loved Razorbacks basketball. He knew there was need for an improved facility when Arkansas moved from the Southwest Conference to the Southeastern Conference in 1992. He also had great respect for Nolan Richardson and all the Arkansas coach had achieved, so he wanted to help.

He called athletic director Frank Broyles and asked for an appointment. "I was nervous," said Broyles. "I wasn't sure what he wanted to discuss. Nolan and I had visited him recently to thank him for all he did for our program. As it was, he asked about our future plans for basketball. I told him we were looking into the cost of expanding Barnhill Arena as well as thinking of a new facility.

"He asked what it would cost to build a new arena. I told him $30 million. He said he would give half and said he was leaving to go hunting."

With that brief exchange, Bud Walton Arena was born. The toughest decision was determining its capacity. At the time, Arkansas was struggling in football and Razorbacks basketball was hot. There was a waiting list for tickets to Barnhill Arena, so Broyles had postcards sent to those on the waiting list, as well as season football ticket holders, to gauge their interest in purchasing seats at the new arena.

After initially thinking 15,000 would be the ceiling, Broyles was astonished by the replies he received. He kept asking the architect to add seats until there were 19,200 seats, including those in the 36 luxury suites (since increased to 47). Season ticket sales skyrocketed and, especially during the first two years in Bud Walton, the place was packed for every game.

Schmidt's Barn

Francis Schmidt was Arkansas' football coach from 1922–28. During that time, he coached two of Arkansas' most famous players. William "Bill" Fulbright won the school's first homecoming game in 1922 with a touchdown and a field goal to beat SMU 9–0. Fulbright later went on to become a very famous United States senator. Schmidt also coached Wear Schoonover, who a year after Schmidt left became Arkansas' first All-American football player after a spectacular season.

Athletic staffs were thin at the time, so when the school decided to start a basketball program, Schmidt was named the coach. Coaching both football and basketball seems an impossibility today, but Schmidt handled both duties well. His football squads were 42–20–3, including 15–3 in his last two seasons. He coached basketball for six seasons and had a glittering 113–22 mark. In fact, his winning percentage of .837 is still the best in school history. There was no NCAA Tournament then but his last four teams won Southwest Conference championships with league marks of 11–1, 8–2, 12–0 and 11–1. In his honor, Arkansas' on-campus basketball home, a modest gym, was called "Schmidt's Barn."

Two decades later, Bud Walton is still one of the finest basketball facilities in the United States. And while the Razorbacks have continually thrived in their palatial home, nothing may ever approach that first season, when the Hogs were undefeated in the building and won the NCAA championship.

"The first time I walked into Bud Walton Arena I thought, *wow!*" said Scotty Thurman, a sophomore during the 1994 campaign who had played his first season in Barnhill. "I was amazed. It was double the space of Barnhill. I wondered if we could fill it and if it would have the same mystique Barnhill had. I wondered how the newness would affect our team. Once we played the first game in there, we were quickly at a comfort level."

After dispensing of Murray State in the first game, Arkansas' Dedication Game came against Missouri, a power in the Big 8 and perennial out-of-conference rival. The Tigers would later go undefeated in their conference and advance to the Elite Eight of the NCAA Tournament, but that night they were no match for the Razorbacks.

"We knew we could beat Missouri, but didn't know it would be that bad," Thurman said. "We hit everything we put up that night." The final score was 120–68.

Arkansas went on to win the national title, then finished second at the NCAA Tournament in the first two years it played in Bud Walton. Even though the Hogs haven't matched those first two seasons, they have won over 80 percent of the games they've played at the arena named after its incredible donor.

59 Reynolds Razorback Stadium

Arkansas finished in the top 20 of the Associated Press poll for the first time in 1936, when it won its first Southwest Conference championship. The Hogs finished in the top 20 again in 1937. With the program on the rise, it was obviously in need of a new facility. Even during the Great Depression, the university was able to construct Razorback Stadium. It opened with a capacity of 13,500 in 1938.

Fred Thomsen was the coach at the time, and his passing philosophy was ahead of its time. One of his quarterbacks, Jack Robbins, was a first-round choice in the NFL Draft. His top receiver, Jim Benton, was not only an All-American at Arkansas, he went on to become one of the top two receivers in the NFL.

But Robbins and Benton were gone when the new stadium opened, and World War II soon drained universities all over the country, including Arkansas, of many of their prime athletes. So, despite its newness, Razorback Stadium wasn't exactly filled to capacity until years later, when John Barnhill was hired as coach and athletic director shortly after World War II concluded.

Under Barnhill's direction, 2,500 seats were added in 1947. In 1950 another 5,200 seats and a new press box were added to the west side. There were 5,200 seats added to the east side in 1957 and expansion projects in 1965 and 1969, the pinnacle of Frank Broyles' years as head coach, increased capacity to more than 42,000.

The Hogs were winning, fans were coming, and the nation noticed. NBC nationally televised the 1965 Texas game from Fayetteville. The Longhorns were No. 1 and the Razorbacks were No. 3. Hall of Fame announcer Lindsey Nelson handled the play-by-play.

Texas was No. 1 and Arkansas 2 for the Big Shootout at Razorback Stadium in December 1969. President Richard Nixon landed by helicopter on the practice field midway through the first quarter and enjoyed the rest of the game along with future president George H.W. Bush and other dignitaries.

By 1985 it was time for another expansion. New seats and the first skyboxes brought capacity to 50,000.

When Arkansas entered the SEC, it was woefully behind in stadium size and amenities. A gift from the Donald W. Reynolds Foundation was the catalyst to a quick improvement. Stadium capacity was raised to over 72,000 and luxury suites were added on both sides. With 132 suites, Arkansas had more than any college stadium in the country.

"We had to have the suites to bring revenue that would allow us to compete in the SEC," Broyles said. "The income from our skyboxes allowed us to bring in as much money per game as some of the SEC schools that had 80,000 seats. We couldn't match stadium size, but we were able to produce the resources necessary to have an outstanding program in the SEC."

The stadium concourses are filled with historic displays, and the video scoreboard was the largest of its kind when it was installed. Its size has since been surpassed, but a recent renovation increased the video space to restore it to the top 10 in college athletics.

60 Running Through the "A"

Fans know it's game time at Reynolds Razorback Stadium or War Memorial Stadium when the University of Arkansas band starts to play "Swing March," as it forms a large "A" on the field. The band moves south, then marches back north to be in position to greet the Hogs when they come running onto the field.

Usually led by the head coach, Razorbacks players race through both ends of the bottom of the A, then converge in the middle of the field before heading for their sideline. The band plays the Arkansas fight song, and the roar of the fans can be heard for miles.

As the UA and opposing captains meet for the coin toss, the band exits the field and it's almost time for kickoff.

For the players, it is an electric moment. When seniors face the prospect of playing their final in-state game, they ponder what it will be like to run through the "A" for the last time. Likewise, on the day high school seniors sign their letters of intent with the Razorbacks, they are often asked if they have thought about running through the "A" for the first time.

Lou Holtz fondly remembers the first time he ran through the "A." So does Bret Bielema, who came to Arkansas from Wisconsin and had heard fans call the Hogs at every Razorback Club meeting he attended. It's different, though, when the team runs through the "A." It's emotional.

Like calling the Hogs, running through the "A" is a time-honored Razorbacks tradition. (AP Images)

It is regarded as such a high honor for the team that athletic director Jeff Long initiated a plan to honor those who have made significant contributions with time, talent, or treasure to the UA athletic program to walk through the "A" just before the team takes the field. The honored guests then greet the players as arrive.

Running through the "A" is an Arkansas tradition that no player or coach ever forgets.

61 Gary Anderson, Bowl MVP

Gary Anderson was the most electrifying Razorbacks runner of the Lou Holtz era. He burst on the scene as a freshman, when he sped around the Texas flanks for a touchdown that started the Razorbacks toward a 17–14 victory at Little Rock, Arkansas' first against the Longhorns in eight seasons.

The '79 Razorbacks, with a blend of talented seniors and terrific freshmen, finished the regular season 10–1 and faced Alabama in the Sugar Bowl. The Crimson Tide completed their undefeated national-championship season by defeating the Razorbacks, but Anderson and his teammates felt great about the future. Against the Tide, Anderson rushed six times for 28 yards and caught seven passes for 53 yards.

That Sugar Bowl started a string of outstanding bowl performances for Anderson. Next was the 1980 Hall of Fame Bowl. Arkansas was just 6–5—disappointing to say the least—but managed to earn a spot in the bowl opposite Tulane. It was a spotlight moment for Anderson. The sophomore tailback exploded for 156 yards on only 11 carries, including a 46-yard scoring sprint, and returned a punt 80 yards for a touchdown.

"We didn't win like we had the year before, so we wanted to finish strong," said Anderson. "We did by beating Tulane. We jumped in front and stayed on them. On the punt return, I thought they had me boxed in, but I sidestepped a tackler and went down the sideline. There were some great blocks on the play."

The following year was a little better for the Razorbacks, who finished the regular season 8–3 and were invited to the Gator Bowl against North Carolina. "It was foggy that night," Anderson recalled. "When either team punted, you couldn't see the ball at all.

Brad Taylor made some great throws for us in the fog." Anderson didn't score, but he caught five passes for 85 yards on a soupy night and rushed for 18. The Hogs lost 31–27 to the Tar Heels.

Anderson's senior season was spectacular, even though the Razorbacks were sidetracked by a tie with SMU that kept them from having a shot at the Cotton Bowl. Instead, Arkansas accepted an invitation to play Florida in the Bluebonnet Bowl. "We knew the Bluebonnet Bowl would be the final time our senior group would play together," Anderson said. "We were disappointed with the end of the regular season, but wanted to go out with a win. We knew Florida was good, but we thought we were better."

At halftime the Hogs might have been wondering—Florida led 17–7. Anderson's 16-yard run had given Arkansas its only touchdown in the first 30 minutes. Anderson got the Hogs comeback started with a one-yard dive into the end zone. He eventually ran for 161 yards on 26 carries and caught three passes for 37 yards. The Razorbacks won 28–24, and Anderson was named MVP again.

Bowl statistics didn't count toward a player's season or career statistics then so think what Anderson missed in his career numbers: 50 carries, 363 yards, 15 catches, 175 yards, and a punt return for a touchdown. Had those numbers counted, Anderson would still be among Arkansas' top 10 career rushers 30 years later. He also would rank third in career all-purpose yards ahead of Felix Jones and behind only Darren McFadden and Dennis Johnson.

62 Steve Atwater

Recruited out of St. Louis, where he set school passing records as a quarterback, tall, rangy, hard-hitting Steve Atwater became the best safety in Razorbacks football history. His hits were legendary. During his professional career with the Denver Broncos, he became known as the "Smiling Assassin."

A two-time All-American and three-time All-SWC player, he set a school record that still stands of 14 career interceptions. Among them, he made a key interception in a 1986 victory over Texas that helped the Razorbacks beat the Longhorns at Austin for the first time in 20 years.

Atwater played on teams that went to the Holiday, Orange, Liberty, and Cotton Bowl games. Selected to play in the East-West Shrine Game, Atwater intercepted two passes and was the game's defensive Most Valuable Player. That helped his draft status significantly.

Tall for a safety at 6'4", Atwater was drafted in the first round by the Denver Broncos and spent 10 years there. He was selected for the Pro Bowl eight times and played on Denver's 1998 and 1999 Super Bowl championship teams.

There have been plenty of hard hitters in Razorbacks football history, but none were better in the secondary than Steve Atwater.

63 Quinn Grovey

There could not have been a more perfect quarterback for Ken Hatfield's flexbone offense at Arkansas than Quinn Grovey. Hatfield knew it as he was pursuing Grovey out of Duncan, Oklahoma. Unfortunately, Oklahoma and Oklahoma State thought Grovey would be perfect for them, too.

"We ran a lot of options in high school and I would throw anywhere from 12 to 15 passes a game," Grovey said. "I visited

Arkansas, Oklahoma, and Oklahoma State. Coach Hatfield and his staff were very genuine. I felt comfortable at Arkansas. But living in Oklahoma, there were those who didn't take kindly to me looking out of state.

"OU had just won the national championship with Jamel Holloway, a freshman, at quarterback. I knew I could play earlier in my career at Arkansas. OSU was in the picture, but in the end I chose the Razorbacks."

When Grovey made that decision, he made it for life. He had a brilliant four-year career, playing for teams that won 29 games and two Southwest Conference championships in his first three years. He still lives in Fayetteville, and the 2013 season was his 16th as sideline analyst for Razorbacks football broadcasts.

Grovey redshirted in 1986 and split time with Greg Thomas in 1987. He didn't play at all in the Liberty Bowl that year and on the bus after the game he received what became a brief motivation speech. "Greg was a senior and I figured I would be the starter in 1988," Grovey said. "When I got on the bus, Coach Hatfield was in the front seat. He told me I had to get stronger and throw the ball a lot better if I wanted to be the quarterback the next year."

Arkansas had recruited several quarterbacks and Grovey knew it. He worked diligently in the weight room and on his throwing during the off-season. It paid off. The Razorbacks won their first 10 games in 1988, lost a two-point nail-biter at Miami, and met UCLA in the Cotton Bowl.

"We were distracted at the Cotton Bowl," Grovey recalled. "We thought Coach Hatfield and his staff were going to Georgia. Plus, we were just happy to be there. It was Arkansas' first Cotton Bowl in 13 years. Our offense didn't show up against UCLA. It was a terrible day for me."

Arkansas had a balanced offense against the Bruins: 21 yards passing and 21 yards rushing in a 17–3 defeat. Grovey, among the fiercest of competitors, was bound and determined to keep that from happening again.

The '89 Hogs started 5–0 but lost to Texas the week before a showdown with high-scoring Houston and its quarterback, Andre Ware. "We were always tight when we played Texas but I couldn't believe we lost to them that year," Grovey said. "We knew we would have to play a perfect game against Houston. They were better than Texas."

And play well the did—Grovey played perhaps his best career game that day. He ran for 79 yards and passed for 256. He threw two deep scoring passes to Derek Russell. He ran and passed for five touchdowns. The Hogs needed them all plus more to defeat Houston 45–39 at War Memorial Stadium in Little Rock. "Ware does a lot of TV games now and I see him every time he does an Arkansas game," Grovey said. "I remind him I was undefeated against him."

Arkansas won out and earned another spot in the Cotton Bowl, this time against Tennessee. Grovey was sick that morning and throwing up in the dressing room. Hatfield wasn't sure Grovey would even play. But he not only played, he directed the Razorbacks to a Cotton Bowl–record 31 first downs as well as 27 points. Unfortunately, it wasn't enough as Tennessee scored 31.

A few days later Hatfield left to become head coach at Clemson. "Coach Hatfield was my man, my coach," Grovey said. "I was sick that he left."

Jack Crowe, offensive coordinator in 1989, replaced Hatfield as head coach. Grovey liked Crowe, too, but few things went right during Crowe's initial campaign. Arkansas had announced it was going to the SEC, but still had to play its SWC schedule. Every one of its Southwest Conference opponents was riled. Then in the second game of the season, against future SEC opponent Ole Miss, the Hogs were stopped inside the 1 on fourth down late in the game to allow the Rebels to escape with a 21–17 victory. Things went downhill from there and the Razorbacks finished the season 3–8.

"I still think about that play all the time," Grovey said. "I don't know how much different our season would have been had we scored, but I think we would have done much better."

Grovey didn't have the size for the NFL, but when he finished college he was Arkansas' career leader in total offense. He has used his degree wisely, and stays close to the program through his radio work.

"I love the Razorback program," Grovey said. "I love the interaction with fans on our pregame show. I love being part of the broadcast team. It's like family. I'm glad I made the decision I did to come to Arkansas."

64 Wilson Matthews

"Wilson Matthews was a lovable character," said Bob Cheyne, sports information director at the University of Arkansas when Matthews was the first assistant coach hired by Frank Broyles. Be that as it may, Cheyne may be the only person, including his wife, Martha, who would have described Matthews as lovable. Most saw him more like a Marine drill sergeant although Razorbacks players knew he had a teddy bear interior deep down.

Previous to joining the Razorbacks, Matthews had an incredible string of successful seasons as head coach at Little Rock Central High School. His teams at Central were 111–14–3 and won 10 state championships in his 11 years there. The Tigers won the mythical national championship in 1957, and Central had won 33 games in a row when Matthews left to join Broyles' staff.

"You didn't have to glamorize Wilson's high school record," said Cheyne. "It was unbelievable."

There were those who had lobbied for Matthews to be named the head coach at Arkansas. No doubt he thought about it himself. He and Broyles were opposites in many ways, yet they ended up working together harmoniously for decades. Matthews was a defensive assistant for 11 years, and coached the freshman team when he moved into administration in 1969.

"I've never known an assistant coach as intense as Wilson was," said Cheyne. "He was all over the field at practice. If he couldn't inspire you, then you weren't worth anything. I remember a fight at practice between Bobby Proctor, a defensive back, and Billy Ray Smith, a lineman who became an NFL star. Billy Ray pushed Bobby down and said he was going to whip him. Wilson ran up to Billy Ray and invited to pick on someone his own size, meaning Wilson. Billy Ray backed off."

Matthews loved Arkansas. That is probably why he remained an assistant to Broyles rather than head coaching elsewhere. He invented one of his own favorite songs and sang it after Arkansas' Southwest Conference wins. It was especially pleasing to sing after a victory over Texas. It went to the tune of "The Old Gray Mare": "We don't give a damn about the whole state of Texas. We're from Arkansas."

Jim Lindsey, who played on the Razorbacks teams that won 22 in a row, loves to tell the story about the pregame prayer before the 1964 Texas game at Austin. "Coach Broyles had us huddled on the field but he was nervous," Lindsey recalled. "He said he was going to lead the Lord's Prayer. He started, 'Lord, I lay me down to sleep' and realized the mistake he had made. He said, 'You take it, Wilson.' Coach Matthews wasn't exactly known for his prayers, but he was quick to finish. He said, 'If I die my soul to keep. Beat Texas! Amen.'"

Once Broyles became athletic director in 1973, Matthews became his most trusted assistant. He was in charge of fund-raising and started what eventually became the Razorback Foundation. Arkansas' method of asking for contributions from its season ticket holders became a national model that has been expanded considerably but still exists today.

Even after he was given emeritus status, Matthews loved to visit football practice and share his insights with whoever happened to be lucky enough to sit with him that day. When his beloved wife, Martha, died, Matthews spent considerable hours with then-head-coach Danny Ford. Ford invited him to watch film, and the two had many conversations about fishing and cooking.

Matthews died in 2002, and Broyles spoke about what a friend he had lost. "Wilson was as loyal as a man can be," Broyles said. "He was loyal to his family, to his friends, to his former players, to me, and to the Razorbacks."

65 Scott Bull to the Immortal Teddy Barnes

Here's the scene: Texas A&M was 10–0 in 1975, ranked second nationally and had handed Texas its first Southwest Conference defeat of the season a week before meeting Arkansas in Little Rock. A victory over the Hogs would send the Aggies to the Cotton Bowl. Arkansas was 8–2, but had only one SWC loss. A victory over the Aggies would create a three-way tie for the league title and send the Razorbacks to the Cotton Bowl as a result of the league's tiebreaker formula.

"Texas A&M had the best defense in the country," said Scott Bull, Arkansas' starting quarterback against the Aggies. "They had Ed Simonini and about eight other defensive players who made it in the NFL. It seemed like they had six or seven shutouts that year."

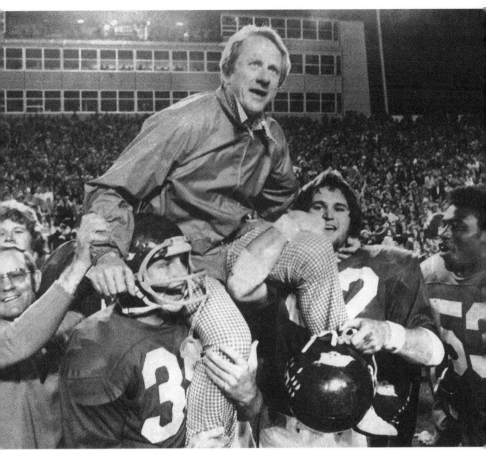

Teddy Barnes (left) and Richard LaFargue carry coach Frank Broyles off the field after the Razorbacks' 30–6 victory against the Aggies. (AP Images)

It was all defense in the first half, until an Aggie punt traveled only one yard, giving Arkansas possession at the A&M 41 with less than two minutes left in the second quarter of a scoreless tie. On second-and-3 from the 34, A&M's Lester Hayes barely missed intercepting a Scott Bull pass. Then Bull ran for a first down on the next play.

With 40 seconds left in the half, Arkansas facing second-and-8 from the 28 and nearly everyone in the stadium thinking the Hogs were setting up a Steve Little field-goal attempt, Bull and Teddy Barnes made the play of their careers.

Barnes was squeezed between two Aggie defenders in the end zone when Bull's pass came in his direction. He leaped and somehow came down with the ball. Touchdown! The Hogs grabbed the lead just seconds before halftime.

"Texas A&M's defensive backs jumped at the wrong time," Bull recalled. "At the top of his jump, Teddy caught it in the back of the end zone. I don't remember if I even saw him open. I threw it into the area where I thought he would be. I was just about to be hit when I let go of the ball."

The second half was all Arkansas. Michael Forrest scored a touchdown. Johnnie Meadors recovered an Aggies fumble in the end zone for another TD. Little kicked a field goal. Meanwhile, the Aggies could do nothing against a strong Razorbacks defense. The Hogs won 31–6 to earn a spot in the Cotton Bowl.

Bull completed only four passes in the game and Barnes' TD reception was his only catch of the contest. Yet it was the most remembered play of Bull's career and by making the catch Barnes became "the immortal Teddy Barnes."

66 Lunney to Meadors

Arkansas and Alabama had only a short history when the Razorbacks visited Tuscaloosa in 1995. The Crimson Tide had won the national championship following each of the first three seasons when it played the Razorbacks. Alabama trimmed the Hogs in the 1962 Sugar Bowl to remain unbeaten. (The Tide already had clinched the 1961 national title since bowl games weren't considered in the final polls at the time.)

Following the 1979 season, Alabama defeated the Razorbacks in the Sugar Bowl. It was another undefeated season for the Crimson Tide, who earned the national championship. It was also the final national crown for legendary Crimson Tide coach Paul "Bear" Bryant.

And in the Razorbacks' first season as an SEC member, Alabama came to Little Rock and trounced the Hogs. That team went undefeated and won the national title.

Their next two meetings were no better. Alabama whipped the Razorbacks in 1993 and 1994—although the '94 Hogs closed the gap considerably, losing just 13–6 at Fayetteville. Still, few could see the Razorbacks beating the Tide on their home turf in 1995, especially since Arkansas had lost its season opener to SMU just two weeks earlier.

"I played late in the game against Alabama my freshman year [1992]," said Barry Lunney, a senior starter at quarterback in 1995. "Their defense was intimidating. By the time I came in they were probably tired from chasing Jason Allen, our starter, so hard."

Lunney had some success throwing the ball in that matchup, and even threw a pass for Arkansas' only touchdown in the game. Three years later, he was a much more confident quarterback, despite the loss to SMU. Arkansas had bounced back from the loss to the Mustangs to smack South Carolina the following week.

"During my career, the 1992 Alabama team was the best I saw," said wide receiver J.J. Meadors, who would break a 24-year-old record for receptions in a season in 1995. "The 1995 season was the first time I really felt we had a chance to beat Alabama."

Lunney said, "Alabama's stadium has more aura than any other in the SEC. Winning at Tuscaloosa is difficult for any visiting team."

The game started well for the Razorbacks. Madre Hill rushed for 87 yards in the first quarter and propelled the Hogs to a 10–3 lead. But by halftime, Alabama had rebounded to move ahead 17–10. A safety made it 19–10 and Alabama might have been on its way to an easy victory when UA linebacker Mark Smith intercepted a pass and returned it deep in Tide territory. The Hogs managed only a field goal, but had successfully turned the momentum.

It was still 19–13 in the fourth quarter when the Razorbacks got the ball at their own 43 with a little more than three minutes left. On the first play, Meadors had the defender beat, but he misplayed the ball in the air and the pass fell incomplete. Shortly thereafter, the Hogs faced fourth-and-16.

"Barry was about to be sacked when he found Anthony Lucas open," Meadors recalled. The play worked for 31 yards, giving Arkansas another set of downs deep in Alabama territory. Lunney hit Meadors at the Alabama 3 and it was first-and-goal.

Three plays netted nothing and the Razorbacks were once again in need of a big fourth-down play. Meadors made it. Lunney rolled to his left and fired a pass low into the end zone. Meadors, only 5'6", went to his knees and grabbed the pass inches from the ground.

"I jumped up and saw the official signal touchdown," Meadors said. "I didn't realize how close it was until we got back to Fayetteville and saw it on [film]. Everyone, including the sports-writers, was asking if I caught it. When I got home and saw the highlights, I could see why people were asking about it. But that ball did not hit the ground. I got my hands under it."

The play happened with just seven seconds left in the game. The ensuing extra point gave Arkansas a 20–19 win.

"That win got us over the hump in belonging in the SEC," said Lunney. "We won the Western Division that year and became the first team from the West other than Alabama to play in the SEC Championship Game."

67 Joe Adams Punt Return

Perhaps the most widely seen Razorbacks play of the YouTube generation was Joe Adams' spectacular punt return against Tennessee in November 2011. Tennessee was going through a difficult year. The Razorbacks, on the other hand, were very good and expected to win the contest. Nonetheless, it was only 7–0 Arkansas late in the first quarter when Adams worked his magic.

It was a high punt and Tennessee's coverage looked good as Adams received the kick at his own 40-yard line. He started to his right but was confronted by a trio of Volunteer tacklers. So he retreated to his left, all the way back to the 31-yard line.

Adams was hit by a would-be tackler at the 31 but bounced back to his right toward the Arkansas sideline. He somehow avoided two tacklers at the 30, then started upfield. Once he got a block and eluded another tackler at the 40, he was off to the races. Adams streaked down the sideline to complete a 60-yard play that seemed more like 80. In all, he slipped by six tacklers.

Razorback radio play-by-play announcer Chuck Barrett said to his partner Keith Jackson and the network audience, "Keith, I just saw it, but I'm not sure I believe it!"

ESPN2 had the telecast. The return concluded with just 17 seconds remaining in the first quarter. The Hogs ultimately won the game 49–7. Adams caught a touchdown pass later in the game, but his punt return was the highlight not only of the matchup but of the entire day's action in college football. It replayed on *SportsCenter* long into the night and the next morning.

YouTube was already a major distributor of video by 2011, so it was little surprise that the play went viral. Hundreds of thousands of fans watched it over and over again. In fact, it's still easily found online and continues to attract viewers.

Adams was an excellent receiver and an incredible punt returner during his Arkansas career. During the 2011 season he returned 19 punts for 321 yards and scored four touchdowns. He even had a TD return in his last collegiate game, a victory over Kansas State in the Cotton Bowl. His longest punt return was a 97-yarder against Ole Miss in 2010. Rarely does a return man even catch the ball as deep as his own 3, much less return it—but Adams' 97-yard runback is the longest punt return in UA history.

68 Robert Farrell Sneaks Behind Them

The hottest pass-catch combo in Arkansas high school football during the early-to-mid-1970s was undoubtedly quarterback Houston Nutt and wide receiver Robert Farrell of Little Rock Central. Both were must-have recruits for the Razorbacks. For Farrell, the decision to become a Razorback came quickly. Nutt wavered between the Hogs and Alabama before becoming the last player Frank Broyles signed as head football coach.

Both were freshmen in 1976. They both saw playing time that year, Nutt when starting quarterback Ron Calcagni was hurt and Farrell in spot duty. Broyles retired, Lou Holtz was named head coach, and Nutt transferred after a year. But Farrell became a prime target—even if he didn't exactly have blazing speed.

"They didn't exactly time me with an hourglass, but for some reason I was regarded as slow," Farrell said. "Our other receivers may have been a little faster but I ran a 4.6 in the 40, which was good for that time. And I did have the ability to get open deep."

Farrell made two of the biggest catches during Holtz's first three years by getting behind the secondary. Somehow he managed to get away from defenders who were faster than he was.

The first was against Texas A&M in 1977, Holtz's first year. Arkansas' only loss had been to Texas, and Broyles—then the athletic director but also a color analyst for ABC—had a week away from the network. He spent the game lobbying two Orange Bowl scouts on behalf of the Razorbacks.

Texas A&M had an outstanding team, and the game was tied at 20-all in the fourth quarter. That's when Farrell struck. "Coach Holtz called an out-and-up pattern," Farrell recalled. "It was the second time in the fourth quarter he called it with me. I was open the first time, but Calcagni threw short to Donny Bobo for a first down. The cornerback broke on the out route. I turned my head like the ball was coming, then planted my foot and went deep. The safety took another receiver, leaving me wide open."

Farrell made the catch and finished the 58-yard play for the touchdown that made it 26–20. Even Holtz took notice of Farrell's lack of blazing speed.

"When Coach Holtz talked to reporters after the game he said he felt good when he saw me catch the ball with 1:42 remaining," Farrell said. "He thought I would run out the clock."

Farrell didn't take that long, of course, but even after the Hogs botched the extra point try, they held on for the victory that, with the help of with Broyles' lobbying, convinced the Orange Bowl to invite the Razorbacks.

Two years later Farrell struck again. The Hogs fell behind Baylor 17–0 early in their 1979 homecoming game before launching a comeback. With the game tied, again at 20-all, Farrell ran the same route and caught a long pass from Kevin Scanlon for the game-winning touchdown. A few weeks later the Razorbacks were invited to the Sugar Bowl.

So even though his speed made him seem slow to many of his teammates, it was Farrell sneaking behind the defensive backs of Texas A&M and Baylor that landed the Razorbacks in two important bowl games.

69 Cissell's Kick Beats Texas

Frank Broyles' second team won nine games and shared the Southwest Conference championship, but failed to beat Texas. They headed to the Gator Bowl, where the Razorbacks defeated Georgia Tech. Broyles knew if the Hogs were going to be a national contender down the line, they would have to find a way to beat Texas.

Broyles also knew that beating UT was essential for Arkansas to have credibility with recruits in Texas. That being the case, Arkansas' 1960 victory at Austin was a landmark win for the program.

It wasn't easy. The Hogs fell behind 14–0 before George McKinney rallied the Razorbacks with a pair of touchdown passes. Texas regained the lead with a field goal, then pounced on a fumble at the UA 1-yard line and scored a play later.

Trailing by nine, McKinney marched the Hogs 69 yards downfield, completing the fourth-quarter drive with a scoring pass to Jarrell Williams (who would later become one of the most legendary high school coaches in Arkansas). With one chance left to win, the Razorbacks drove again, this time to the Texas 12. With 25 seconds left, Broyles called on his kicker, Mickey Cissell.

"The wind had switched and was behind his back," Broyles recalled. "It wasn't that long, but he kicked it low and I wasn't sure it was going to make it."

Bob Cheyne, sports information director at the time, said, "It barely made it over the crossbar. It wasn't pretty, but it was sure a big field goal for the Razorbacks."

It was big for several reasons. First and foremost, it brought national credibility to Broyles' program. The victory over Texas launched the Hogs to a league title and the host spot in the Cotton Bowl. And it gave the Razorbacks the ability to lure young players in the Lone Star State.

"Beating Texas opened a recruiting pipeline into the state of Texas," Broyles said. "It helped us get players like Ronnie Caveness and Glen Ray Hines, who were a major part of our national championship teams."

Cissell's kick, no matter how pretty it may or may not have been, also gave the Hogs the assurance that they could win at Texas. After a narrow 7–3 loss in 1962 at Austin, the Hogs beat Texas in its home stadium in 1964 and 1966. It was no small feat. The Razorbacks were the only team to have a winning record against Texas in games played in Austin during the decade of the 1960s.

70 Ronnie Caveness

While sophomore defensive lineman Loyd Phillips was on his way to becoming one of the most famous players in Razorbacks history, and the 1964 Hogs were loaded with terrific players, there is no doubt that the ringleader of the defense—which had shut out its last five regular-season opponents—was linebacker Ronnie Caveness.

Caveness was from Houston and became one of the first great players who Frank Broyles recruited from that state. The Hogs had to beat out Alabama for his services. In fact, Caveness had signed a Southwest Conference letter of intent with Arkansas and a Southeastern Conference letter with Alabama. He didn't have the nerve to call Crimson Tide coach Bear Bryant to tell him he was going to Arkansas.

A consensus All-American in 1964 and two-time All-SWC selection, Caveness is still the only Razorback to have made more than 20 tackles in a game more than once—and he did it four times. He set a school record that still stands of 29 single-game tackles, against Texas in 1963. He made another 25 tackles against the Longhorns in 1964.

It was a Caveness interception that turned the tide in an important win over Tulsa in 1964. The Hurricane had a terrific quarterback named Jerry Rhome and jumped to a 14–0 lead. Tulsa was driving again when Caveness intercepted a halfback pass. Arkansas' offense got going after that and eventually the Razorbacks earned a 31–22 victory. It led to an unbeaten, national championship season.

The key win that year was against defending national champion, Texas. The Hogs needed every one of Caveness' tackles to hold off the Longhorns 14–13.

"After we beat Texas, our defense was very confident," Caveness said. "We became a different team. We shut out everyone after Texas before our final game against Texas Tech. [The Longhorns] had just one loss and would have gone to the Cotton Bowl if they beat us. But Bobby Roper blocked two field goals, we shut them out, and went to the Cotton Bowl to play Nebraska."

Caveness started at center and linebacker as a sophomore before settling full-time at linebacker when teams went to separate groups on offense and defense. His school-record 357 tackles was broken five years later by Cliff Powell, but since then no one else surpassed it for another 38 years.

Madre Hill

When Madre Hill returned a kickoff 100 yards for a touchdown against LSU in the regular-season finale of his freshman season, he displayed the dazzling potential that led schools all over the country to recruit him out of Malvern. Having won him, the Hogs knew they had a special back.

Hill showed just how remarkable he was in 1995, his sophomore campaign. The Razorbacks were 4–7 in 1994 and suffered a shocking defeat at SMU in the '95 season opener. In his third year as head coach, Danny Ford needed someone to inspire his team. Ford reinserted senior Barry Lunney Jr. at quarterback and turned Hill into a workhorse.

"I didn't think we would lose a game in 1995," Hill said. Then in the first game of the season. SMU kept grabbing my face mask and they beat us. I thought, *Okay, if that's the way it's going to be, I've got to step up.*"

Hill stepped up big time. A week after the SMU loss, Hill set a school record and tied the SEC best by scoring six touchdowns in a victory over South Carolina. He torched the Gamecocks for 178 yards on 31 carries. It wasn't a surprise when Hill was named SEC Offensive Player of the Week.

"I wanted to lead the SEC in rushing that year," Hill said. "Robert Edwards of Georgia had scored five touchdowns the same week we lost to SMU. I was thinking to myself I needed to score six touchdowns."

Three weeks later he was SEC Offensive Player of the Week once again when he became only the sixth Razorback to rush for at least 200 yards in a game. He hit 200 on the button with 29 carries

Madre Hill racks up some yardage during his record-breaking 1995 season.
(AP Images)

in a win at Vanderbilt. He also scored two touchdowns against the Commodores.

As Hill was emerging, the Hogs were surprising the SEC. After a loss to Tennessee, quarterbacked by Peyton Manning, Arkansas needed a victory over Ole Miss. In a hard-hitting defensive battle at Memphis, Hill burst 71 yards for the game's only touchdown and the Razorbacks won 13–6.

Incredibly, a win over Auburn in the next game would clinch Arkansas' first-ever SEC Western Division title. Hill was ready for the showdown in Little Rock. He carried and carried and carried. When it was over he had set a school record with 45 carries and had earned 186 yards and a touchdown in the Hogs' 30–28 win. The SEC picked him as Offensive Player of the Week for the third time.

Hill had six 100-yard rushing games in 1995 and helped the Hogs earn a spot in the SEC Championship Game against Florida. It became obvious how dependent the Razorbacks were on Hill after he suffered a knee injury in the first quarter. Arkansas never recovered; the Hogs lost not only to Florida, but to North Carolina in the Carquest Bowl.

Hill rushed for 1,387 yards in 1995, a school record until Darren McFadden broke it 11 years later. He missed the 1996 and 1997 seasons with torn ACLs on both knees but recovered to play in 1998. His speed wasn't quite the same but he still had 100-yard rushing efforts against Alabama and Kentucky.

"I really enjoyed the 1998 season playing for Coach [Houston] Nutt," Hill said. "I wasn't in great shape. My knee was okay, but I was 18 pounds heavier. But he took the pressure off me. It was like a total new start with him."

Arkansas has had some tremendous running backs during its illustrious football history, but only McFadden has ever had a season to exceed Hill's 1995 campaign. And it might be a long, long time before anyone is the SEC Offensive Player of the Week three times in the same season again.

The Burls Way

Brandon Burlsworth was a very good offensive lineman at Harrison High School before becoming a Razorback. Danny Ford was Arkansas' coach at the time, but the Hogs recruited Burlsworth only casually.

"I remember visiting with Brandon in his living room," said Louis Campbell, an Arkansas assistant coach at the time who was assigned Burlsworth. "I thought to myself, *This kid will never play. Was I ever wrong about him.*"

Ford didn't offer Burlsworth a scholarship, but gave him the opportunity to walk on and redshirt before competing for playing time. Few players ever have taken such advantage of a redshirt year. Burlsworth dropped nearly 60 pounds of mostly baby fat and gained it back in muscle.

Burlsworth's work ethic earned him notice—and a scholarship. After serving as a backup offensive guard in 1995, he earned a starting spot in 1996 and remained locked into his position for three years. In fact, he started 34 consecutive games.

"His work ethic was extraordinary," said Houston Nutt, head coach during Burlsworth's senior year. "I remember one night when we finished our staff meeting and we were about to leave. I heard something in our indoor workout area. When I went to see what it might be, there was Brandon, working on his technique. He wanted a little more practice. There were very few like him."

Burlsworth helped Nutt's first team win nine games, and he earned All-SEC and All-America honors. His black, heavy-framed glasses became his trademark.

During his time at Arkansas, Burlsworth was totally focused. It was faith, family, academics, and football—and nothing else. He was determined to not let anything detract him from his goals. He earned his bachelor's degree in marketing management during his junior year of eligibility. By the time his Razorbacks football career was over, he had completed his master's degree requirements. In fact, he was the first Razorbacks football player ever to earn a master's degree before playing his final game.

Drafted in the third round by the Indianapolis Colts, Burlsworth died eleven days later in a one-car accident while driving to Harrison to pick up his mother for church. The Razorbacks football family was stunned. Because of the incredible example Burlsworth had set in academics and going from walk-on to All-American, Nutt recommended Burlsworth's jersey No. 77 be retired. Athletic director Frank Broyles agreed. It remains one of two numbers retired by the team.

Years later, Burlsworth's locker remains in the UA dressing room as he left it as a reminder of his legacy. His brother, Marty, and wife, Vicki, started the Brandon Burlsworth Foundation, a charity that has benefitted thousands of young people in Arkansas, particularly in the area of vision care. Although Brandon lost his life in 1999, his example of living life "the Burls Way" endures today.

73 Houston Nutt

The last high school football player to sign a letter of intent with Frank Broyles when he was Arkansas' football coach, Houston Nutt also became the Razorbacks' head football coach in December 1997. Nutt's coaching career turned out much better than his playing career did.

Although Nutt started at quarterback in three games during his freshman year, he served as a backup for most of his two seasons before transferring to Oklahoma State. A native of Little Rock, he returned to Fayetteville as an assistant on Jack Crowe's staff in 1990.

As head coach at Murray State, then Boise State, Nutt always wanted to return to Arkansas as head coach. When he got his opportunity, he didn't disappoint. After the Hogs had gone 4–7 in the two years before his arrival, Nutt took the Razorbacks to nine victories in 1998. Only a late fumble in a heartbreaking loss to Tennessee kept Arkansas out of the SEC Championship Game that year.

Nutt had a close relationship with Broyles and spent a decade in Fayetteville as head coach. Eight of his 10 teams played in bowl games and six won at least eight regular-season games. His teams annually ranked among the SEC leaders in rushing, leading the conference several times. Over the years he coached Darren McFadden, Cedric Cobbs, and Felix Jones—three of the top five career rushers in Arkansas history.

He also coached quarterback Clint Stoerner for two seasons. Stoerner led the Hogs past Texas in the Cotton Bowl in his final game at Arkansas and finished his career in possession of most of the school's passing records (those have since been broken).

But it wasn't all strawberries and cream for Nutt. When Nebraska courted him for its head coaching vacancy a few Hogs fans weren't happy. The following year his name was tossed around for the LSU job, hurting more of his support at home. There was also the 2006 season—which should have been one of his happiest, when the Hogs won 10 games in a row, earned a spot in the SEC Championship Game, and were selected to play in the Capital One Bowl—when internal strife caused some difficulties.

Nonetheless, the Hogs bounced back with a strong 2007 in which McFadden was Heisman runner-up for the second year in a row. The regular season ended with a bang: a victory over top ranked LSU in three overtimes at Baton Rouge. But with Broyles departing as athletic director, Nutt knew his time was up. He resigned after the LSU game and three days later was head coach at Ole Miss.

"We loved our time at Arkansas," said Nutt. "It was my dream job. I grew up in Little Rock and was a ball boy at War Memorial Stadium. I will always have fond memories of my time as Razorback head coach."

74 Bret Bielema

When Jeff Long hired Bobby Petrino as head coach in December 2007, he thought he had a long-term solution to taking Razorbacks football to a championship level. After four years, including two of exhilarating success, Long had to dismiss Petrino for off-the-field behavior, leaving the Hogs without a coach in the spring of 2012.

At that point, Long knew he couldn't lure a big-time coach because few coaches are willing to move in April. Instead he brought back John L. Smith—a former head coach at Louisville and Michigan State who was on Petrino's staff—as interim head coach for the 2012 season. The results were disappointing: 4-8. But at least Long had a head start on hiring a permanent replacement, and he knew just what he was looking for.

"Just as when we hired Bobby Petrino, we had to hire a coach who was tough enough to come into this league," Long said. "There were a number of assistant coaches who were interested, but our program deserves a sitting head coach."

With an entire state watching but Long giving no clues, the Arkansas athletic director pulled a rabbit out of his hat when he lured Bret Bielema from Wisconsin.

"Bret's record on the field—three straight Big Ten championships and Rose Bowl appearances—was outstanding," said Long. "I also knew him as a person and knew he cared deeply about the players. He could be characterized as a players' coach, but at the same time he had discipline, accountability, and an academic focus. He demonstrated that from the day he arrived at Arkansas. He has a high level of expectations for the players and will not compromise, whether they are starting players or walk-ons."

Bielema's incoming coaching record was exceptional, but so was his reputation for academic achievement. "Bret has had tremendous academic success, including a great APR [academic progress rate] rating at Wisconsin," Long said. "In today's athletics, if a coach doesn't understand the importance of that academic piece, he is not going to be a success on the field. He will lose players and they won't be matriculating as juniors, seniors, and fifth-year seniors. Bret understood that. He proved it at Wisconsin and has brought the same mentality to Arkansas.

"There is a toughness a coach has to have mentally and physically in this conference and I think Bret brings that to us. With time, as he builds the program his way, without cutting corners, we are going to have a proven winner here."

Bielema's first year wasn't what he or anyone else expected, but the foundation was laid for long-term success for Razorbacks football.

The First Team

Twenty-five years after the first college football game between Princeton and Rutgers, the University of Arkansas fielded its first football team. The schedule was the most unique in school history. There were two games against a group representing Fort Smith High School (many of the players were adults) and one against Texas at Austin. It was the second year for football at the University of Texas.

John C. Futrall, a Latin professor, agreed to be the first coach. He lasted three seasons and had a record of 5–2; all five wins were against the Fort Smith team. Arkansas lost to Texas and Drury, a school in Springfield, Missouri. Futrall would later become university president, a title he held for 26 years. All the while, he was very supportive of the football program.

There were only 14 players on that first team. They were quarterback Wright Lindsey, halfbacks W.W. Haydon and Arthur J. McDaniel, fullback and star player Herbert Y. Fishback, ends Edward Mook and H. Dade Moore, tackles Raleigh Kobel and LeRoy Campbell, guards Tommy H. Rogers and J.C. Braswell, and substitutes Jim Brown, E. Carney, and W.S. Norman.

With so thin a squad, it was no wonder Arkansas, then nicknamed the Cardinals, lost so convincingly at Texas. Even in the program's infancy, the Longhorns were deeper, bigger, stronger, and faster than almost any opponent it played.

Not much else is known about the 1894 Cardinals except that which was gleaned by then Bob Cheyne, who brought three of the school's first players back for a football game in 1953.

"It was the 60th year for Razorback football, so I tried to find out if any members from the first team were still living," Cheyne said. "I found three of them. One was in Dallas, one was in Houston, and one was in Forrest City. I invited them back for a game and they all came.

"They brought pictures, articles from scrapbooks, and other things with them. They were thrilled to be remembered and to be able to share their memories of the first games played at the University of Arkansas. They told me about the decision to play the game at Texas. Coach Futrall had to make a decision about whether to take a flat fee to pay for travel or a percentage of the receipts.

"As it turned out, Futrall took the flat fee and didn't quite make expenses. They had a good crowd for the game, about 1,500, and the gate percentage that was offered turned out to be better than the guarantee."

Cheyne continued corresponding with the three original Arkansas players for several years afterward. "They were grateful for the trip to Fayetteville and appreciated being introduced to the crowd. They were in their eighties at the time. I'm really glad we brought them back."

What would they think today if they walked on the UA campus? They would never recognize the place—nor would they believe how important football has become to Arkansas and throughout the United States.

76 All-Century Team

At the conclusion of the 1993 football season, the 100th in the history of the University of Arkansas' program, athletic department staff members, with assistant athletic director Bill Gray

Lance Alworth (23) sprints through the Ole Miss secondary on his way to All-America honors.

spearheading the process, decided to poll Razorbacks fans to name an All-Century Team.

There was great interest throughout the state and anticipation was high for the results. The All-Century Team was invited to the 1994 Red-White spring football game to be introduced to the fans. Most of them were able to make it.

There were some no-brainers among the roster, but the competition at several positions unleashed a variety of opinions because there were so many good choices. When the ballots were collected, here were the winners:

Offensive Linemen: Bud Brooks (1954 Outland Trophy winner), Freddie Childress, Leotis Harris, Glen Ray Hines, Steve Korte, and R.C. Thielemann.

Receivers: Jim Benton, Bobby Crockett, Chuck Dicus, and Wear Schoonover.

Running Backs: Lance Alworth, Leon Campbell, Barry Foster, Jim Mooty, and Clyde Scott.

Quarterbacks: Joe Ferguson, Quinn Grovey, Lamar McHan, and Bill Montgomery.

A side note on the offensive roster: it must be remembered that the All-Century Team was named before the days of Darren McFadden, Felix Jones, Cedric Cobbs, and Fred Talley, who changed the dynamics of Arkansas' career rushing chart. Somehow Ben Cowins and Dickey Morton, the top two rushers in school history at that point, didn't get enough votes to rate on the team. Two of the receivers, Benton and Schoonover, played before 1940 but were All-Americas and remained legendary figures more than 50 years later.

The All-Century Team's defense:

Linemen: Dan Hampton, Dave Hanner, Wayne Martin, Loyd Phillips (1966 Outland Trophy winner), Billy Ray Smith Sr., Billy Ray Smith Jr., and Fred Williams.

Linebackers: Ronnie Caveness, Wayne Harris, Cliff Powell, and Dennis Winston.

Secondary: Steve Atwater, Alton Baldwin, Martine Bercher, Ken Hatfield, and Billy Moore (also an All-American quarterback).

Kickers: Steve Cox, Steve Little, and Pat Summerall.

There weren't as many notable omissions on the defensive side, but somehow kicker Kendall Trainor, who made 24 field goals in a row in 1988, was inexplicably left off. Schoonover, Benton, and Scott were the only pre-1950 players on the squad.

When the next All-Century team is picked in 2093, will there be enough historians around to remember McFadden, Jones, Ryan Mallett, Tyler Wilson and others who would have been stars more than eight decades before the balloting takes place?

77 Eating at Herman's and Mary Maestri's

During the early days of Arkansas' football success, there weren't many restaurant choices in the tiny community of Fayetteville. The franchises that now populate College Avenue and Martin Luther King Jr. Boulevard weren't around until the late 1970s. Even then there weren't many choices for a night out on the town.

Springdale had the AQ Chicken House, and residents of northwest Arkansas flocked there for the fried chicken that was rated best in Arkansas. Tontitown had the Venetian Inn, which was like eating in an open ranch atmosphere. The steaks covered your plate and the spaghetti was homemade. The fried chicken was good, too.

While AQ and the Venesian Inn were packed before and after Razorbacks football games, the lines were longest at Herman's and Mary Maestri's. Herman's advertises itself as a rib house, but also offers steaks and chicken. Back then, the place seated 60, maybe 70 people and whatever you ordered took a while. The cook? Herman.

Herman Tuck opened the restaurant in the 1960s. If he ever did anything to enhance the appeal of the exterior, it was not noticeable. A plain white building, you wouldn't think to stop at unless you knew what was inside.

The steaks were fabulous. The sides were slaw and Texas Toast no matter what was ordered. The atmosphere was terrific.

"I always enjoyed our times at Herman's," said CBS announcer Jim Nantz, who made several trips there when he visited Fayetteville to do play-by-play for telecasts of games featuring some of Nolan Richardson's best teams. "One of the last trips my dad took with me before he had Alzheimer's was to Fayetteville and we ate at Herman's then went to see *Dumb and Dumber*. It was a wonderful time."

Herman would sneak in certain media people on the nights before games, but otherwise the wait could be over an hour. Either way, it was well worth it.

Mary Maestri's was in Tontitown, just east of the Venetian Inn. It was more on the elegant side and was run by Danny Maestri, Mary's grandson. Salad and tortellini came with any meal ordered and were delicious appetizers. All the pasta was homemade. It was best to order spaghetti instead of a baked potato with steak or chicken. The rolls alone were worth the trip.

As was the case at Herman's, the lines were long on the night before a game or following an afternoon kickoff—which was all Arkansas had before installing lights in the late 1980s. Mary Maestri's also was the choice of the Southwest Conference press tour, when media from Texas and Arkansas traveled during August to all the conference's schools.

There were some pretty hilarious happenings on the tour. One night John Hollis of the *Houston Chronicle* barked like a dog while crawling under the table after maybe one glass too many of Mary Maestri's wine. There's no telling what Arkansas' Frank Broyles, who never indulged in alcohol, must have thought.

The good news for Razorbacks fans today is both restaurants are still in business. Herman sold the place but the menu remains the same. So does the atmosphere. It's a little pricier, but isn't everything?

Mary Maestri's has since moved. The original was torn down after more than 60 years in Tontitown. It's now near the corner of Highway 412 and East Robinson Avenue in Springdale. A few items have been added to the menu, and there is a charge now for the tortellini, but Danny Maestri still greets his guests just like he did 30 years ago.

78 Radio at the Catfish Hole

The Catfish Hole on Wedington Drive is one of the best restaurants in Fayetteville, northwest Arkansas, and the entire state for that matter. The catfish is delectable and the hush puppies can't be beat. It's a fabulous place to eat on Friday night before a game or for pregame lunch or postgame dinner.

But the Catfish Hole is more than just a great place to eat. It's *the* place to hang out with the head football coach on Wednesday nights during the regular season.

"We were looking for a place to do a call-in show with Bobby Petrino when he became the head coach," said Todd Curtis, who worked for the Arkansas Razorback Sports Network, then transitioned to Razorback Sports Properties when IMG purchased Razorbacks radio rights. "Pat Gazzola, the owner of the Catfish Hole, suggested having it in his Razorback Room. Pat said people would come for the food and the coach.

"Coach Petrino agreed to do it there. The first year was good, and the audience continued to grow. The year Arkansas went to the Sugar Bowl it was packed for every show. There was a waiting list. We put over 200 people in that room. There wasn't a place for another person."

Chuck Barrett, radio voice of the Razorbacks hosts the show. He recalled, "That Sugar Bowl season people would make reservations for the next week while they were there for the show. If it was already sold out they would make reservations for the next date with an opening.

"Bobby brought players with him and it was a chance for fans to see the personality of the coach and players. They really enjoy that. It is a lot of fun."

After Petrino was dismissed, interim coach John L. Smith did the show at the Catfish Show for a year. Despite Smith's engaging personality, the lack of success during the season "turned the event into a ghost town," according to Curtis. "At times we might only have [had] 50 people there."

Things picked up again after Bret Bielema became the permanent head coach. Barrett noted, "Bret is great personally with fans. Generally he's the last to leave. He will sign every autograph and pose for every picture until every fan has finished. He didn't bring players his first year because of the practice schedule but he would take questions from the audience that were unscripted. It is good engagement with the fans."

Barrett enjoys the show because "there's a lot of energy in the room. It's a simple show to host but you can't help but be energized. It's a great place for fans to see the coach on a more personal level."

So if you are in Fayetteville on a Wednesday night during football season, make your reservations early and enjoy listening to Chuck and the coach at the Catfish Hole. The reservation features an all-you-can eat buffet and a guaranteed seat. And if it's Friday before a football game and you are hungry, the Catfish Hole is the place to be. You might even see a recruit or two.

79 Dean Weber

In March 1973, Dean Weber became the head athletic trainer at the University of Arkansas. He served as trainer for 35 years then worked diligently in the athletic department as the director of equipment operations. He moved to the Razorback Foundation in the spring of 2014.

"I had been the assistant trainer at North Carolina for five years and knew I needed to make a career move if I wanted to be a head trainer," Weber recalled. "I visited with Coach [Frank] Broyles by phone and he offered me the job. My wife at the time wanted to visit the campus. Coach Broyles told me North Carolina had trees and mountains and Fayetteville had trees and mountains. He would pay me $500 more if I would accept without visiting. That was a lot of money back then, especially when the job paid $10,000."

Weber obviously liked Fayetteville; he's never left. Along the way, he has built relationships with four decades of UA athletes. "I've taped tens of thousands of ankles," Weber said. "I had a lot of fun doing it. Belonging to a team and building relationships is wonderful. I know there is a business side, but it's still a game. We had a great time. Of course, it helped that we were winning."

The Hogs were winning and winning big during Weber's time as trainer. He served teams that played in 26 bowl games. "The Orange Bowl after the 1977 season, when we beat Oklahoma, was definitely a highlight," Weber said. "I have memories of a lot of big wins. The 1989 Houston game in Little Rock may have been the best football game I've ever seen. It was back and forth all night before we finally won."

Yet Weber's favorite moments are when players come back to see him. He said, "I had a player from the 1990s come back just the other day. When he was a player he was really struggling with a lot of things. He said he remembered coming to talk to me and I helped him. He remembers that. Since then he came back and got his degree and he's working on a master's. There are quite a few athletes like that."

In dealing with injuries, Weber had a major scare only once. It happened in 1988, when quarterback Quinn Grovey was knocked out in the Texas A&M game at Fayetteville.

"It's the only time I ever thought a player was dead," Weber said. "When he first went down he was as lifeless as you can be. It scared me. By the time we got to him he was starting to recover and, of course, he did. He didn't come back in that game, but two weeks later he was ready for Miami."

Grovey holds Weber in highest regard. He said, "When I think of Dean Weber, the word that comes to mind is…'legend.' He is so respected by players past and present. Dean is one of the best ambassadors for the university when it comes to players staying connected and involved. I know players who will come to Fayetteville just to visit Dean and no one else. I'm proud to call him my friend. I can count on Dean any and every time."

Houston Nutt, whose ankles were taped by Weber for two seasons as a player and who later worked with Weber for 10 years as Razorbacks head coach, said, "When I was hired as coach, Dean congratulated me, then asked if I wanted him there. I said 'of course.'

"There are very few trainers who spend that many years still wanting to tape players' ankles. Most want to delegate. But Dean had a tremendous relationship with the players. There was a bond. He talked their language. At practice he would see that they were a little too tired and ask me to cut practice short. He gave me information that helped me make decisions on what foods we would eat, our travel plans, and even who should be roommates on the road."

Weber was involved with travel plans for years. He conceded, "We had our share of foul-ups. If you do it long enough, a plane will be late or break down. For the most part, though, everything worked fine.

"We worked with some great people. For years our team would stay at the Ramada Inn in Conway before Little Rock games. Those people were so good to us and always friendly. They treated us like family. We finally outgrew it. During Houston's 10 years [at head coach] our team stayed at the Clarion Inn in Bentonville before Fayetteville games. They were always great to work with."

A member of several halls of fame, including the Razorback Sports Hall of Honor, Weber still loves going to work every day, even after four decades that have made him "a legend."

Mike Nail

Mike Nail grew up in Fayetteville—and of course he listened to Razorbacks football radio broadcasts. Bob Cheyne was the "Voice of the Razorbacks" at the time, Nail was inspired by his example. "Bob Cheyne was my inspiration," said Nail. "He made me want to be the Razorback announcer. He had a distinctive voice, and it was obvious he loved what he was doing. I listened thinking that was what I wanted to be."

Nail's time came in 1981. Paul Eells was the radio voice for football and basketball but also was sports director of KATV in Little Rock. KATV began televising so many basketball games that it became necessary to have Eells step aside from the radio job.

"I gave [basketball coach] Eddie Sutton and [athletic director] Frank Broyles tapes of high school basketball games I had done

Power Outage

Mike Nail vividly remembers Arkansas' victory over top-ranked and undefeated North Carolina in a 1984 game at Pine Bluff. Of course, Nail remembers the game—but he also recalls how he broadcast Charles Balentine's game winning shot. Nail said, "There were about three minutes left in what was a great, great game. Our broadcast was going as normal when someone inadvertently kicked our table and the power went down. We couldn't get our unit to respond. Back then we had a telephone at our table as a backup. I picked up the receiver, dialed our studio and called [in] the last two minutes, including Balentine's shot. It's the only time in 29 years I ever had to do that, and it was in one of Arkansas' biggest moments."

with Sutton as the color man," said Nail. "I also gave them some tapes of my broadcasts of the Oklahoma City 89ers baseball games.

"It went on and on, and finally I asked Coach Sutton if he had heard anything. He told me I needed to go see Coach Broyles. When I went to his office, I didn't even get a chance to ask about it. Instead, he offered me the job. Of course, I accepted."

Twenty-nine years later, in March 2010, Nail announced his retirement. He said that he never dreamed he would be in his position so long. "After I had done the games eight or nine years, Bob Cheyne asked me how long I had been in the position," Nail said. "He told me he did the games for 11 years, so I had a ways to go to catch him. After my 11th year he came to congratulate me. That meant a great deal to me."

But Nail was far from finished after 11 years. He had the privilege of calling Eddie Sutton's games for four years, then every game Nolan Richardson coached for 17 seasons. He also worked all five of Stan Heath's years, then the first three of four seasons with John Pelphrey at coach.

"I worked with some great coaches," Nail said. "Eddie Sutton and Nolan Richardson are hall of fame coaches. Obviously, doing the game in 1994, when Arkansas won the national championship, stands out. So does going to Rupp Arena for the first time, and those three great games we had with Alabama in the first SEC season. The last time Arkansas and Alabama played that year in the SEC Tournament, there were seven future NBA players on the floor, including six first-rounders."

Nail, who has attended Razorbacks games as a fan since retiring as longtime voice, noted, "I've reflected back and am amazed at what good fortune I had. There are a lot of announcers who would do anything to do a game at the Final Four. I got to do *three* Final Fours. That's beyond belief.

"It was a privilege to be the voice of Razorback basketball, particularly during the great years of Eddie Sutton and Nolan Richardson."

81 Chuck Barrett

Chuck Barrett knew he wanted to be "Voice of the Razorbacks" when he was just 15 years old. The desire came from his initial experience at handling play-by-play.

"I grew up in Clarksville, [Arkansas,] and for some reason the guy who did the public address at the Little League games did a play-by-play," Barrett recalled. "One night he was sick. I was 15 and said I would do it. I knew right then what I eventually wanted to do."

Barrett landed his first broadcasting job with a radio station when he was 16 and stayed in the industry continuously, not counting during his freshman year at the University of Arkansas. During his sophomore year he began working full-time for KEZA while also attending school.

While much of his radio work involved covering school board and city council meetings, Barrett spent time doing football and basketball play-by-play for Clarksville, Van Buren, and Alma High School games. He was news director at KMAG in Fort Smith when he got the call he had been waiting for.

"A guy I knew was a friend of Pat Demaree, who owned radio stations in Fayetteville," Barrett said. "The guy who did Razorback baseball [had] just quit, and Pat was looking for someone to host a talk show and do Razorback baseball. I jumped at it."

After a year of discussing politics when he wasn't describing Razorbacks baseball in the first SEC season of 1992, Barrett switched to talking about sports exclusively. In 2001, his program went statewide.

In the meantime, Barrett had joined the Razorbacks football broadcast team in 1994. "I would drive to the old KARN studio in Little Rock every Saturday morning," Barrett remembered. "I would answer the phone during the pregame show, tape highlights, and do the scoreboard show after the games. A year later, the network was looking for a producer. I didn't know what that involved, but I told them I could do it. That's what I did until 2007."

Well known statewide by then, Barrett was an easy choice for football voice of the Razorbacks going into the 2007 season. Longtime voice Paul Eells had died in an automobile accident just before the beginning of the previous season and Mike Nail, who called Razorbacks basketball, subbed for a year before Barrett arrived.

"I was thrilled, scared, and everything in between," said Barrett.

A few years later Nail retired and Barrett became the first broadcaster ever to handle Razorbacks football, basketball, and baseball games.

"I enjoy the changing of the seasons," Barrett said. "There's something neat about football going into basketball and basketball going into baseball. Plus, doing these games has allowed me to see places I had never seen before. That's one of the best aspects of the job."

Nail said, "I love being a fan now. Chuck does an outstanding job with all the sports, but I particularly enjoy listening to him do basketball."

Barrett's most notable call perhaps came in baseball, when he described Brady Toops' ninth inning, two-out grand-slam home run that allowed the Razorbacks to defeat Wichita State and avoid elimination in the NCAA Tournament. Eventually, the Hogs reached the College World Series. "I think that's the first time I realized the notoriety that could come with making a dramatic call," Barrett said. "So many people have told me they remember that call. There are times you prepare yourself for a moment that might be significant, but I wasn't prepared for that one. It was an exciting play to call."

His favorite football call so far has been the 2007 triple-overtime victory over top-ranked LSU in Baton Rouge. And in basketball, he had the privilege of calling Michael Qualls' rebound dunk with less than a second remaining in overtime, which gave the Razorbacks a victory over Kentucky in Bud Walton Arena.

82 Harold Horton

A native of DeWitt, Arkansas, Harold Horton was recruited by coach Jack Mitchell. But he played his entire varsity career for Frank Broyles. He later returned as an assistant football coach, recruiting coordinator, associate director, and finally executive director of the Razorback Foundation.

"My brother, Don, played for Jack Mitchell, then was on Coach Broyles' first team," Harold recalled. "I was on the scout team that year [1958]. We took a beating. They worked us hard. They drove us. We still talk about that off-season program. It's hard to describe it to other people."

Clearly, the hard work paid off. Horton played on teams that won or shared Southwest Conference championships in 1959, 1960, and 1961, and the Hogs finished in the top 10 nationally all three years.

A few years later Horton was named an assistant coach and worked with Arkansas linebackers. He coached some great players during his tenure but was most highly regarded as a scout. He knew the back roads of Arkansas and recruited several prospects from small towns that few others knew about.

He remained on staff when Lou Holtz replaced Broyles as head coach, but was fired after the 1980 season. Deeply hurt, he went into private business before becoming head coach at the University of Central Arkansas.

"Lou Holtz told me later that he had fired several coaches during his career, but there were two he never should have fired and I was one of them," Horton said. "I told him he didn't need to apologize to me. Actually, he got me out of a rut I didn't know I was in. I never would have had the opportunity to coach at UCA if Lou hadn't fired me."

At UCA, Horton compiled an amazing record that included sharing two Division II national championships. At the same time, Ken Hatfield was enjoying success as head coach of the Razorbacks. But after the 1989 season, Hatfield left to become head coach at Clemson and Jack Crowe was elevated to head coach from his offensive coordinator position. At that time, Broyles and Crowe asked Horton to return as recruiting coordinator and he did so.

"A lot of people thought I was crazy," Horton said. "But I made the right decision because of the way Coach Broyles supported me when I came back. When Jack Crowe was going to lose his job, and before it became public, Coach Broyles came to me and told me not to worry about my job. He said I would have a job at Arkansas. He did that when Jack, Danny Ford, Joe Kines, and Houston Nutt were gone. He never put me in a bind. I have a lot of respect for Coach Broyles because of the way he treated me."

Even when Broyles retired, Horton remained at the Razorback Foundation. Jeff Long, who replaced Broyles as athletic director, knew how important Horton was because of his connections with so many people in the state.

Horton finally retired and has no regrets. "I've lived a blessed life," Horton said. "The University of Arkansas and the people of Arkansas have been very good to me. It has been special to be a Razorback."

83 Dennis Winston vs. USC

Dennis Winston was a relatively unknown sophomore linebacker for the Razorbacks at the beginning of the 1974 season. Amazingly, he was recruited by Arkansas and other schools despite the fact that his high school didn't field a football team during his senior year! His freshman collegiate class was only the second to be given eligibility by the NCAA since World War II, and he had already lettered. By the time the Hogs finished upsetting fifth-ranked Southern California in the '74 season opener, Winston had gained national recognition.

USC was loaded and had defeated the Razorbacks two years in a row. The Razorbacks went just 5–5–1 in 1973 and were rebuilding with a solid group that would win a Southwest Conference title in 1975. Winston was one of the team's promising young players.

War Memorial Stadium was packed, as always, for the 1974 opener and Razorbacks fans roared throughout the contest. Ike Forte, a speedy junior-college transfer, got the Hogs off to a great start with a 27-yard touchdown burst.

The Trojans answered quickly as All-American Anthony Davis returned the ensuing kickoff 106 yards for a touchdown. But that would be it for the Trojans.

Davis and USC quarterback Pat Haden became very well acquainted with Winston, who made tackle after tackle. Haden—who later played several years in the NFL, was a commentator on college football telecasts, and became athletic director at USC—said later, "It was the worst game I ever played. Arkansas dominated us."

That's exactly what happened. Haden completed only six of his 18 passes and had four of them intercepted. In all, the Trojans earned just 59 yards through the air. Even with Davis, USC managed just 154 rushing yards; meanwhile, the Razorbacks ran for 262.

Steve Little kicked two field goals and Mark Miller ran a quarterback sneak for a one-yard touchdown to give the Hogs a 20–7 fourth-quarter lead. It became 22–7 when Haden was forced out of the end zone for a safety late in the contest.

Winston, who would become an All-Southwest Conference linebacker, made 19 tackles, including 11 unassisted, against the Trojans that day. He was named National Defensive Lineman of the Week. Most important, he helped the Razorbacks earn one of their biggest upset victories in history with his amazing effort against the Trojans.

"It was one of the best games of my career," Winston said. "We had prepared for USC and I was assigned to stop Anthony Davis. I did my job. Of my 19 tackles, I think all or almost all of them were on him."

Winston later enjoyed a terrific NFL career, including seven seasons with the Pittsburgh Steelers, who won two Super Bowls during that time. Winston gained plenty of notoriety during his time with the Steelers but he never forgot that USC game.

"The USC game put me on the map," said Winston. "We beat the No. 1 team in the country. It was their only loss that year. Over two months later, Davis scored six touchdowns against Notre Dame. We really felt good about what we'd done after that."

84 The Bequettes

Several families have University of Arkansas legacies. Brothers Harold and Don Horton both played football for the Razorbacks. James, Sam, and Eusell Coleman were offensive linemen between 1916 and 1927. They were never on the same team, but all three captained the Razorbacks for at least one season. Then there are the Hatfields, Dick and Ken, who both played for the 1964 national championship team. On the basketball side, Ron Brewer and his son Ronnie were both great at Arkansas and then the NBA.

No doubt there are many others, but none like the Bequettes. George played for the 1954 Southwest Conference champions that met Georgia Tech in the Sugar Bowl. His son Jay played on an SWC co-championship team that went to the Sugar Bowl and faced Alabama. Jay's brother Chris played on an Orange Bowl team, and Jay's son Jake helped the Hogs earn a spot in the Sugar Bowl, Arkansas' first-ever BCS appearance.

"That's pretty neat, but our record was pretty ugly," said Jay. "We were 0–4 in those games. That's not very good."

Defensive end Jake Bequette represented the third generation of football-playing Bequettes at Arkansas. (AP Images)

Well, maybe not, but it took a lot to get to those games to begin with. The '54 Hogs finished 8–3. Jay played on teams with a four-year record of 34–13–1 and played in three other bowl games, winning two. Chris' years were spent with teams that were 35–13–1 and played in four bowl games. Jake's squads were 34–17 and played in the Sugar and Cotton Bowls. Jay was All-Southwest Conference. Jake earned All-Southeastern Conference honors.

"We are born-and-bred Hogs," said Jay.

George was first in line. He grew up in a factory town in Missouri and knew an athletic scholarship and the education that went with it were his only escape from a life spent in the factory.

"Dad took advantage of his education at Arkansas," said Jay. "He earned his degree and later earned a master's from the University of Kansas. He worked for State Farm Insurance and made sure all of us knew how important education was.

"He was an inspiration to Chris and me. He was very outgoing. He was a hardworking, passionate guy. He was old school and told us plenty of stories about that 1954 team." The '54 Hogs were called the "25 Little Pigs" because they weren't that big and not many of them played.

"Dad loved the coach, Bowden Wyatt," Jay said. "In fact, Dad visited Coach Wyatt in Knoxville after Wyatt became coach at Tennessee. Wyatt wanted my dad to transfer but he didn't.

"Dad also loved Bill ["Groundhog"] Farrell, the trainer. Dad didn't cry much, but you could get him to cry when he started talking about Groundhog. Another guy he loved was Bob Cheyne, who was the sports information director.

"He loved John Barnhill, who was the athletic director, too. Barnhill used to come out and watch practice almost every day. Back then when you broke the huddle you ran to the line of scrimmage. One day Dad broke the huddle and ran right over John Barnhill. He felt terrible and tried to help him up but Barnhill said,

'I don't need your help. I've been run over by bigger and better players than you.'"

Jay was never pressured to go to the University of Arkansas, not even when he was being recruited in the winter of 1979 and his dad's Missouri license plate read, HOGS 79. George wore No. 79 when he played at Arkansas and that was Jay's freshman-year jersey number at Fayetteville.

"I looked at other schools, including Missouri, but Arkansas was the best school for me," Jay said. "Our freshman group was a cool group of guys. Lou Holtz was compelling to play for. There was nothing boring about him. It's hard to believe we could win 10 games that first year with so many freshmen starting on defense. Billy Ray Smith started at tackle and only weighed about 210 that year. We played Alabama in the Sugar Bowl. They were men.

"We had four good years. We didn't have a deep class, but there were 10 or 12 pretty accomplished players. Three of them were among the top 32 players drafted after our senior year. It was a salty group."

Jay graduated in December of his senior year. In January he started law school. He earned his law degree and currently practices in Little Rock.

Chris was next. He was a freshman in 1983 and redshirted. He had been recruited by Lou Holtz but spent his entire career playing for Ken Hatfield. He kept everyone loose with his sense of humor and contagious laugh. He graduated in three years and worked on his law degree during his final two years of eligibility.

"Those last two years were tough on Chris," Jay said. "He was a starting offensive lineman and had to take a full load of law school classes. He would get about four hours of sleep a night."

Chris has done a variety of things since graduating and now lives in Little Rock, where he has a company called American Coaches Wealth Management.

Last in line—at least to this point—was Jay's son Jake. He played four years for Bobby Petrino. A terrific defensive lineman, he made 23.5 career quarterback sacks, the third highest total ever by a Razorback. He currently plays for the New England Patriots.

"Recruiting was different for Jake," Jay said. "[High school] players can commit so much earlier now than we could. He was offered a scholarship in April before his senior year and accepted. He always wanted to go to Arkansas.

"I was very proud of him and enjoyed watching him play for the Razorbacks. I knew how hard he worked. He earned his degree in finance in three years and is a paper away from finishing his master's in sports management. We go to Boston two or three times a year to see him play."

So what's next for the Bequette clan? "We would love to see grandchildren playing at Arkansas, but want them to do whatever they want," said Jay. Is there a fourth generation ahead?

85 Three Overtimes at LSU

Houston Nutt was in his 10th year as Razorback head football coach when athletic director Frank Broyles, who had recruited Nutt as a player and hired his as head coach, announced he would retire at the end of the year. The Razorbacks, blessed with three of the greatest running backs in school history—Darren McFadden, Felix Jones, and Peyton Hillis—had won 10 games in 2006 but were 7–4 going into the regular-season finale at Baton Rouge against top-ranked LSU. Nutt knew things weren't looking good.

Nonetheless, Nutt and his staff prepared diligently for the day-after-Thanksgiving date with the Tigers. Somehow, the Razorbacks were more than ready.

"For some reason LSU and Alabama always brought out the best in us during my time as coach at Arkansas," Nutt said. "We always gave our best effort in those games. LSU was the closest thing in the SEC we had as a rivalry. David Bazzel had created the Boot, a big trophy that went to the winner of the game. Our players always wanted that trophy in our museum, not LSU's.

"When we played LSU, I always felt if we were up three or down three, even up six or down six in the fourth quarter, we would win."

The game went back and forth all day. Arkansas led 7–6 at intermission, but no one could have predicted what would happen after halftime. Both teams scored a pair of touchdowns in the third quarter. LSU added a two-point conversion to tie the game. Arkansas' touchdowns came on a 73-sprint by McFadden and a 65-yard run by Hillis.

In the fourth quarter McFadden took a direct snap, faked a run, and hit Hillis with a pass for what turned into a 24-yard touchdown play. LSU rallied to tie and the game went overtime.

"The reason we were so good in overtime was because we practiced it so much," Nutt said. "We ran plays in practice after we were tired. We would put the ball on the 25 and run a series, just like in overtime. We did it all the time. It's one of the best things we did as a coaching staff."

Overtime was tense. LSU scored a touchdown in the first overtime and Arkansas was facing fourth-and-goal at the Tigers 10. "We called a wheel route for Hillis," Nutt explained. "Casey Dick, our quarterback, was under duress and had to throw it a little early. Hillis made a great catch for a touchdown. It was the play of the game. If we don't score on that play, the game is over."

McFadden scored next for the Hogs but the Tigers tied it again. Then it was Hillis blasting into the end zone followed by a two-point run by Jones. LSU scored a touchdown but needed a two-point conversion to force a fourth overtime.

"We already had the offense huddled to start the fourth overtime," Nutt said. "Then Matterral Richardson intercepted the two-point try. The game was finally over. It was a great play and it gave our entire sideline the greatest feeling."

Chuck Barrett was in his first season as radio play-by-play man. He said, "It was the greatest game in any sport I've ever seen. It was back and forth. It was as if McFadden and Hillis were saying, 'Can you top this?' Then Richardson intercepted that pass. It had been a tough year for the team and everyone who worked around them, but that was one thrilling moment.

"It was also a thrill to see how quickly Tiger Stadium could get empty and how quiet it could get. That was very cool."

It was the last hurrah for Nutt. Two days later he resigned. Shortly afterward, he was named head coach at Ole Miss. The coaching change overshadowed one of the greatest games in Razorbacks history.

86 Dedication of Frank Broyles Field

Frank Broyles had announced in February 2007 that he would retire as athletic director on December 31. It would complete 50 years with the University of Arkansas for Broyles as football coach, then athletic director.

To honor Broyles it was decided to name the football field after him. The dedication took place on November 3, when the Razorbacks hosted South Carolina. Actually, festivities began early, as lettermen who played for Broyles gathered the evening before the game to salute their former coach.

A young Frank Broyles celebrates one of his 144 victories as Razorbacks football coach.

The dedication ceremony took place at halftime. By then the Razorbacks and Gamecocks had been taking turns racing up and down the field on each other.

"I've gotten to know and be friends with Steve Spurrier and he told me he had never seen anything like the running backs we had then," said Houston Nutt, Arkansas' coach who also concluded his Arkansas tenure that season. "Tyrone Nix, their defensive coordinator, said Darren McFadden, Felix Jones, and Peyton Hillis were electrifying. They couldn't stop them."

The Razorbacks led 28–10 at the half, and the lovefest for Broyles began. Surrounded by his family and many former players, Broyles received a thunderous ovation as well as a surprise. Keith Jackson, his longtime broadcast partner during his days as color analyst for ABC, came to Fayetteville and gave a special greeting over the public address system. Broyles was deeply touched.

"I didn't know he was in the stadium," Broyles said, "but I sure recognized that voice as soon as he said the first word."

It was a major celebration in front of 70,000 fans—but it wasn't the end of the merry-making. The Razorbacks won 48–36

The First SEC Game

Arkansas announced it was joining the Southeastern Conference on August 1, 1990, but football schedules are set long in advance. Thus, it was determined that 1992 would be the Razorbacks' first to play football in the SEC. By the time the Hogs got around to playing South Carolina, the conference's other new addition, in the second game of the season, another school from South Carolina had already sent shock waves throughout Arkansas—and the country, for that matter.

In the 1992 opener, Arkansas lost a 10–3 decision to the Citadel. Perhaps the quietest group of Razorbacks fans in history left Razorback Stadium speechless. One of the most bizarre weekends in school history continued the next day with firing of Jack Crowe as head coach. Later that day, Joe Kines, the veteran defensive coordinator, was named interim head coach.

Kines was a fireball. He spent the next week in practice sprinting between the offense and defense, encouraging both units at the top of his lungs. If he was exhausted by Saturday, he didn't show it; neither did the Razorbacks.

With Jason Allen directing the offense and Orlando Watters returning a punt and an interception for a touchdown, Arkansas smashed South Carolina 45–7 at Columbia. And with that, the Hogs were 1–0 as an SEC member. When it was over, the players carried Kines off the field on their shoulders. It was one of only three victories that year but it was an auspicious beginning in the SEC for the Razorbacks.

and McFadden tied the SEC rushing record with 321 yards. Battery mates Jones earned 166 yards—including touchdown runs of 40, 72, and seven yards—on just 13 carries and Hillis added another 35 yards on six touches. McFadden capped the scoring with an 80-yard run and also tossed a 23-yard touchdown pass to Robert Johnson.

"It was a great night," Nutt said. "It was great for Coach Broyles and great for the Razorbacks. During the game Darren McFadden told me, 'Coach, I'm in a zone,' so we kept giving the ball to him.

On a normal night McFadden would have earned the game ball. But on that day, it belonged to Frank Broyles as the field he coached so frequently on was named after him.

87 Jeff Long

Jeff Long had been on the University of Arkansas campus only once before becoming a candidate to replace the retiring Frank Broyles as athletic director. But his first visit left a lasting impression.

Long was an assistant athletic director at the University of Oklahoma and joined other administrators in his department on a visit to Fayetteville to study the upgrades and expansion that had been done to Reynolds Razorback Stadium.

"I had no idea what northwest Arkansas looked like," Long said. "Norman[, Oklahoma,] was flat, so that is how I envisioned Fayetteville. When we got there we saw trees and hills. It was a beautiful area. Then we got to view the athletic facilities and I thought they were incredible." Little did Long know then that he would eventually become the UA athletic director.

He officially assumed the position January 1, 2008, after leaving his job as AD at the University of Pittsburgh several months ahead of time, leaving time to move himself and his family to Fayetteville and learn as much as he could about the Razorbacks program before Broyles left office.

Long learned quickly. His first thoughts? "The facilities were remarkable and the University of Arkansas, northwest Arkansas, and Fayetteville, Arkansas, offered everything my family was looking for," Long responded. "It was an opportunity to come to the most competitive conference in America and join a university that was growing and expanding in academic reputation.

"Also, the passion of the fan base is unique. I've been in a number of different places and everybody thinks they have the most passionate fan base. But I really believe that because of the state pride, because we are the flagship institution, and because even students who go to UCA, Arkansas State, Henderson State, and the other colleges in Arkansas are still Razorback fans, I believe our fan base is the most passionate in the country.

"There is a tremendous passion for everything Razorbacks in our state. That's particularly refreshing, exciting, and exhilarating for someone who has been AD in a pro market, where you have to scrap to get people interested in your program. We don't have that problem at Arkansas and I love that."

While the facilities Long inherited were among the best in the country, as other schools updated and expanded their facilities, the Razorbacks had work to do as well. Long has directed the construction of a new football building, the Fred W. Smith Football Center, a new baseball-track indoor workout facility and a basketball practice facility scheduled to be ready in the summer of 2015. A new academic center and north end zone expansion of the Reynolds Razorback Stadium are also on the horizon.

"Arkansas' facilities were ahead of most schools when Coach Broyles was here, but other schools saw what Arkansas had and over time they built up," Long said. "That put us in a position where we needed to do more. That's the nature of our business."

In his first six years on the job. Long had to hire two football coaches—Bobby Petrino and Bret Bielema (John L. Smith was also an interim coach for a year)—and a basketball coach, Mike Anderson. He combined men's and women's athletics into one department rather than two and utilized increased revenue to expand the budget from slightly more than $50 million to nearly $80 million.

"I hope people remember that our upgrade in facilities and everything else we have done was focused on the student-athletes in our program, and that we built facilities that helped them be the best they can be as an athlete, as a student, and in growing to be the people they want to be. In the end that leads to championships, graduations, and young people who go on to have great lives."

88 Visit Crystal Bridges

Okay, it's not Razorbacks-exclusive, but if you are in northwest Arkansas for a University of Arkansas sporting event and you would like a touch of culture, a visit to Crystal Bridges Museum of American Art is a must.

The brainchild of Alice Walton, daughter of Walmart co-founder Sam Walton, the museum isn't far from downtown Bentonville and the headquarters of Walmart. It features an incredible collection of American art, including original portraits of George Washington, and is itself an architectural delight. It's also a beautiful setting, situated in the middle of trees and trails.

Crystal Bridges' goal is to "celebrate American Spirit in a setting that unites the power of art with the beauty of nature." People come from throughout the United States and all over the world to see the fabulous collection of art. There is plenty of Arkansas flavor to the museum as well.

To get there from I-540, take exit 88 and turn west onto Central Avenue, go three tenths of a mile and turn right (north) on John DeShields Boulevard. It becomes Museum Way and leads to the Crystal Bridges parking lot.

For additional information, go to crystalbridges.org or call 479-418-5700. Visitors hours are Mondays and Thursdays from 11 AM to 6 PM, Wednesdays and Fridays from 11 AM to 9 PM, and Saturdays and Sundays from 10 AM to 6 PM. The museum is closed Tuesdays.

While you are in Bentonville, you might head for the downtown square to visit the Walmart museum, which documents the history of the largest retailer in the world.

89 Zach Hocker

When Zach Hocker arrived on the University of Arkansas campus, he wanted to land the punting job. He got a late scholarship offer from the Razorbacks after a kicker from Texas changed his mind about coming to Fayetteville. Little did Hocker know that he would break a scoring record that had stood for more than 40 years.

"They signed me because Dylan Breeding only averaged about 35 yards per punt the year before," Hocker said. "I was confident I could be the punter. But in the preseason, Breeding was nailing it. I knew I might redshirt, but I just wanted the opportunity to get on the field."

Alex Tejada was a senior and Eddie Camara had been signed to challenge Tejada as the placekicker. Late in the preseason, the

Hogs gave Hocker a shot at kicking field goals and extra points. It was all he needed.

"Alex and Eddie both had a bad day in one of our preseason practices and I had a great day," Hocker recalled. "They moved me into the No. 1 spot on Thursday before the first game. I was blessed to have the job from that point on."

Ironically, Hocker and Camara remained friends even though Hocker won the starting spot. Camara transferred to the University of Central Arkansas, where he became the Bears' placekicker.

"Eddie and I are best friends," said Hocker. "When we would have an open date, I would go to Conway and watch his games. If UCA had an open date, he would come to our game. There were no hard feelings."

It would be difficult to have hard feelings toward Hocker when looking at his accomplishments. He made 61 of his 79 field goal attempts, a percentage of .772, and nailed 171 of his 173 extra point tries. He scored 354 points, shattering the school scoring record set by Bill Burnett in 1968–70.

"Bill is with Fellowship of Christian Athletes and we are great friends," Hocker said. "We heckled each other. It was cool to be in contact with him as I approached his record. When I came to Arkansas I never would have thought anything like this would be possible. Even after scoring so many points my first two years I never thought about the record. As I got closer, I definitely wanted to break it."

Burnett said, "Zach has been involved with FCA so I had gotten to know him before he was bearing down on my record. When he broke it I congratulated him and told him I was glad he was the one who broke the record—for two reasons. One, he is from Arkansas and two, he is a Christian."

Hocker not only broke it, he destroyed it. Burnett scored a school-record 49 touchdowns in his three seasons, for 294 points. Steve Little got close, kicking for 280 points and Darren McFadden scored 44 touchdowns (for 264 points), but neither could catch Burnett. Burnett missed half of his senior season and freshmen weren't eligible to play for the varsity during his era. McFadden played three years, then declared for the NFL Draft.

"It's amazing all this happened," said Hocker, who completed his career in 2013. "I am from [Russellville,] Arkansas, and it was a dream come true for me to play for the Hogs. But I knew as early as my first preseason that either Eddie or I would have to transfer. It was cool to stay and do so much."

Hocker also was fortunate to play for high-scoring teams. His first two seasons were under Bobby Petrino, when the Razorbacks played in the Sugar and Cotton Bowl games. He had 222 points by the time his sophomore year was completed.

"When we had Ryan Mallett, then Tyler Wilson at quarterback, we were in position to score almost every time we had the ball," said Hocker. "I was fortunate to play when our offense was so powerful. Even if I didn't have the opportunity to kick a field goal it was easy to tack on a point with a PAT. It was definitely a blessing to be part of that offense."

He fell off considerably, though, as a junior when he made just 11 of his 18 field goal attempts. "I never felt right that year," said Hocker. "The chemistry just wasn't right. We made adjustments, and everything was much better during my senior season."

Indeed, things couldn't have worked much better. Hocker hit 13 of his 15 field goal tries and all 28 of his extra point attempts. He continued to have great success kicking off with 68 percent of his kicks resulting in touchbacks. And with Breeding having graduated, he took over some punting duties, averaging 45.7 yards per kick.

Burnett's record fell early in Hocker's senior season. Extraordinarily humble, Burnett didn't mind seeing his record broken after over four decades, especially by someone as thrilled to be a Razorback as Hocker.

Billy Moore

In the first 121 years of Razorback football, there have been a slew of great quarterbacks. Joe Ferguson, Quinn Grovey, Ryan Mallett, Bill Montgomery, Tyler Wilson, Steve Creekmore, Lamar McHan, and Jack Robbins were among the best in the country during their time at Arkansas. But only one UA quarterback ever has earned first team All-America honors.

Billy Moore was a sensational defensive back and a heckuva quarterback. He took advantage of Arkansas' success in the early 1960s and a terrific sports information director, Bob Cheyne. In 1962, Moore was named to the Football Writers All-America team.

Billy Moore (left) earned first-team All-America honors in 1962, and remains the only Razorbacks quarterback ever to be so honored.

Moore's statistics weren't overwhelming. In 1962, he rushed for 585 yards on 131 carries and completed 51 of his 91 passes for 673 yards. But he produced 19 touchdowns and led the Hogs to a 9–1 regular-season record. It was the first time Arkansas ever had won nine games before the bowls.

"I just told the truth about Billy Moore," said Cheyne. "The guy presented more problems to the defense than any player we had. If you had just one week to prepare for Arkansas and had to defend Billy Moore, he offered you a challenge. You didn't know whether he would go inside, outside, or throw the football. He wasn't known as a great passer, but he was as good as you'd want because he was a great runner.

"I loved working with Billy. He was completely unpredictable. Billy Moore with the football was as dangerous a football player as we ever had."

While Moore's overall statistics aren't comparable to the quarterbacks of today, he set a record that stood for 47 years when he raced 90 yards for a touchdown against Tulsa in a 1962 game. No Razorback ran as far again until Broderick Green went 99 yards against Eastern Michigan in 2009.

91 Shawn Andrews

Relatively unknown before his senior year at Camden Fairview, Shawn Andrews became perhaps the finest offensive lineman ever to play at the University of Arkansas. None of the scouting services had his film and he hadn't made the camp circuit. But when he blossomed as a senior, suddenly everyone took notice.

Fortunately for Arkansas, Houston Nutt and his staff had Andrews on their radar long before most other coaches did. Little surprise, then, that Andrews became a Razorback. He was an instant success.

"He was the most gifted offensive lineman I ever coached," said Nutt. "He was a big guy with great feet. He was spectacular. He had great heart. I first noticed him at an AAU basketball game when he was in the 10th grade. He was so fluid for a big man."

By the fourth game of his freshman football season, Andrews was a starting offensive tackle. He was second-team All-Southeastern Conference that year. In 2002 he became the first Razorback ever to earn first team All-America honors as a sophomore.

He was All-America again in 2003 and was a finalist for the Outland Trophy and Lombardi Award. He won the Jacobs Trophy, awarded to the SEC's top blocker, in back-to-back seasons in 2002 and 2003.

"We had Shawn at right tackle and Jason Peters at tight end," Nutt said. "They were side by side, and we took off. We became very right-handed, but it didn't matter. Those guys were so good that no one could stop us. We led the SEC and were fifth nationally in rushing."

Andrews blocked for Cedric Cobbs, Fred Talley, and quarterback Matt Jones. All three rank in the top eight among Arkansas' career rushing leaders.

After his third season, Andrews declared early for the NFL Draft and was a first-round selection of the Philadelphia Eagles. But his impact in Arkansas was massive. In just those three seasons, Andrews helped the Hogs win 25 games, including nine in each of his last two campaigns.

92 Dennis Johnson

Dennis Johnson set a University of Arkansas and Southeastern Conference record that, without the help of a rule change, is not likely to be broken. Johnson came close to never setting it at all, however—he nearly was not a Razorback.

Although he was an outstanding high school running back from Texarkana, Johnson was not offered a scholarship by Arkansas coach Houston Nutt. However, when Nutt left the Razorbacks and Bobby Petrino was hired as head coach, Tim Horton and Bobby Allen, assistant coaches who were retained by Petrino, convinced the new coach to sign Johnson.

"Bobby Allen was recruiting Texarkana at the time, and he played a big role in getting Johnson to Arkansas," Horton said.

Once at UA, Johnson had some outstanding moments as a running back. He rushed for 160 yards against Ole Miss in 2011, 127 yards versus LSU in 2008, and 107 against Florida in 2009. But his greatest impact was as a kickoff returner.

"Dennis had a great feel for finding the seam," said Horton. "He also broke tackles, something not a lot of return men can do. You would think his return was about to end at the 20, then he would bounce off a tackler and get to the 45."

Johnson returned kicks during his freshman and sophomore seasons, was injured and had to redshirt a third year, then was the lead returner again during his final two campaigns.

"It takes courage to return kickoffs," Horton said. "There are 10 or 11 players running as fast as they can to hit you. Even after the injury Dennis came back and did a great job."

Johnson's best year was his sophomore season, when he returned 40 kicks for a school-record 1,031 yards—an average of

Dennis Johnson's return record will likely remain in the record books forever.
(AP Images)

nearly 26 yards per try! Additionally, he broke his own record 905 yards, which he set as a freshman.

An NCAA rule change made it more difficult for Johnson later and is the reason his SEC mark may never be broken. During his early seasons, kickoffs came from the 30-yard line. In an effort to limit kickoff returns and their dangers of injury, the NCAA rules committee moved kickoffs to the 35. Suddenly there were much fewer returns, as many kicks sailed into the end zone. So it is extremely unlikely that Johnson's total of 2,784 yards on 119 returns will ever be approached.

There won't be as many returns for touchdowns either. Johnson, for his part, went the distance three times. He opened the 2009 season by returning a kickoff 91 yards for a score against Missouri State. It is the only time in UA history that the season-opening kickoff was returned all the way. He had a 98-yard return in a victory over South Carolina in 2011. His most dramatic, though, came against Tulsa in 2008.

In a game that went back and forth, Tulsa had just tied the score. Johnson took the lead back when he returned the ensuing kick 96 yards for a touchdown.

"Our game with Tulsa was tight all the way," Horton said. "Tulsa had just tied it. Momentum had shifted in Tulsa's favor. Then Dennis returned the kick for a touchdown. That was huge for us. It completely changed the momentum."

Now the momentum in college football is for fewer kickoff returns. That's why Johnson's record will likely stand the test of time.

93 The 1981 Texas Game

Arkansas had defeated TCU 22 years in a row when the Razorbacks visited Fort Worth in game four of the 1981 season. The Razorbacks led 24–14 with just more than five minutes to go in the game and the Horned Frogs were on their own 3-yard line. With the help of a Razorbacks fumble, somehow TCU managed two touchdowns and stunned the Hogs 28–24.

"T...C...U," a disgruntled UA coach Lou Holtz repeated over and over in the dressing room. Then he added, "We lost to T...C...U." A shocked group of Razorbacks couldn't afford to even snicker. It may have been funny to think of it later, but in the dressing room it was no laughing matter.

Two weeks later, Arkansas was a considerable underdog when top-ranked Texas came to Razorback Stadium. "Texas was No. 1, but we were confident all week," said Billy Ray Smith at the time. "They had just beaten Oklahoma badly. We thought they might overlook us. I don't know if they overlooked us, but we were ready."

Keith Jackson, legendary ABC announcer, who was assigned to work the telecast, told an observer the day before the game, "Texas may be No. 1, but they are a shaky No. 1. I think they are ripe to upset."

Jackson couldn't have been more accurate. Of course, there was precedent. Texas had come to Fayetteville ranked No. 1 before. In 1965 the Razorbacks beat the top-ranked Longhorns 27–24. Texas won the Big Shootout in 1969 15–14, when the 'Horns were No. 1 and the Hogs were No. 2. Those games were close; the '81 game wasn't.

It should be pointed out the day was overcast from the beginning. ABC gambled on a late kickoff. They tested conditions at 6:00 and 6:30 PM and believed they could make things look good—even though Razorback Stadium didn't have lights at the time. Kickoff was set for 2:45 PM.

Perhaps it was an auspicious beginning as Smith recovered a fumble at the Texas 20 on the game's first play. Gary Anderson, who had burned the 'Horns in 1979 and again in 1980, scored for a 6–0 lead. On Texas' next possession, a snap over the punter's head sailed out of the end zone for a safety. Things got progressively worse. Quarterback Tom Jones lofted a scoring pass to Anderson just before half. By the time the fourth quarter began, the Hogs led 39–3. The final score was 42-11, Arkansas' most lopsided win ever over its arch SWC rival.

Arkansas played suffocating defense and had superb field position all day. By the middle of the third quarter, the only question about the game's outcome was whether or not it would finish in daylight. Texas passed more than 50 times, a school record at the time, and, with many of the tosses incomplete, the clock stopped frequently.

With darkness setting in and the game nearing the finish, Razorbacks fans rushed the south end zone to tear down the goal posts. However, there was still time on the clock. Holtz, fearing a penalty despite the lopsided score, raced to the scene and insisted the fans leave the field.

It took a while to clear the celebrants, but the game resumed, practically in the dark. When the game finally concluded, the fans returned and down went the south goal posts. It was one of only two times—the 1992 Tennessee game was the other—when fans tore down the goal posts in Razorback Stadium.

Beating Texas in the Cotton Bowl

When Arkansas left the Southwest Conference for the SEC, it left its greatest in-conference rivalry behind. So whenever Arkansas met Texas, Razorback fans treated the event as much more than just a game. State pride was at stake when it came to playing the Longhorns.

Hogs fans fondly remembered the last game the schools played in the SWC. A huge underdog, Arkansas upset the 'Horns 14–13 in Little Rock in 1991. When Arkansas announced it would join the SEC, SMU was the only former SWC member that would schedule games with the Razorbacks. No one knew if Arkansas and Texas would ever play again.

But at the end of the 1999 season, it happened. Arkansas was invited to take the SEC's spot in the Cotton Bowl and Texas was selected to represent the Big 12. Longhorns fans may or may not have been enthused about the matchup, but Arkansas fans bought every ticket they could find.

"You had to grow up in Arkansas to realize how big the Texas game was," said Houston Nutt, a Little Rock native who was in his second year as UA head coach in 1999. "I remember Lou Holtz, when he was coach, couldn't understand why our fans put so much emphasis on that game. The people of Arkansas look at the University of Texas as 'the mighty giant.' It may be just another game to Texas, but it was like the Super Bowl to Arkansas fans."

Nutt admitted he was nervous before the game. "Coach Broyles had allowed us to move to another hotel the night before the game so we could have a quieter environment," Nutt said. "I was having trouble getting to sleep. Coach Broyles called me and told me to just relax. He knew we had a good game plan. He told me to just go out and have fun the next day. After he hung up, I fell right asleep. That call meant a lot to me."

When the clock struck midnight, a new millennium began as it turned to January 1, 2000. It also signaled a new era in the Arkansas-Texas rivalry.

It was a typical Razorbacks-Longhorns standoff in the first half, as each team managed only a field goal. Nutt was still a little nervous—until he entered the locker room at halftime. "Everything changed at the half," Nutt recalled. "It was a small dressing room. A bunch of our linemen were sitting together and they said, 'Coach, we've got 'em. We're more physical than they are.'

"We didn't change much on offense. Our defensive coordinator, Bobby Allen, said he would bring more pressure since their quarterback couldn't run. In the second half, Cedric Cobbs took off and Clint Stoerner made a huge play off our goal line."

Arkansas broke the tie when Stoerner hit Cobbs with a short pass that the Hogs freshman running back turned into a 30-yard touchdown. Cobbs scored again on a 37-yard blast and Mike Jenkins added a 42-yard TD jaunt. By the time the game ended, Arkansas had a 27–6 win.

Allen kept his end of the bargain, too. The Hogs sacked Texas quarterbacks eight times, and the Longhorns finished with an astounding –27 yards rushing. It was the most futile rushing effort in Texas' illustrious history.

"When it was over I did something I probably shouldn't [have], but I was caught up in the moment," Nutt said. "Most of the Texas fans were gone and our fans were still there, so I flashed the upside-down Hook-'Em-Horns sign. That didn't go over too well in Texas, but as someone who was born and raised in Arkansas, it was something I had seen our fans do many times when we beat the Longhorns.

"[Then-Texas-coach] Mack Brown and I are friends now, and that has given me a chance for him to understand. I wish I hadn't done that, but it sure felt good to beat Texas."

The game remains the only time Arkansas and Texas ever have played in a bowl game, so the Razorbacks are undefeated against Texas in the postseason.

95 Broyles vs. Bobby Dodd

Before he became a coach, Frank Broyles played for Bobby Dodd at Georgia Tech. He was a terrific quarterback, and in 1944 set an Orange Bowl record for passing yards that wasn't broken for more than 60 years. After starting his career as an assistant coach at Baylor, then going to Florida, Broyles joined Dodd's staff at Georgia Tech and enjoyed an amazing run at what would now be called offensive coordinator.

"Frank had one of the greatest offensive minds in the game," said Bob Cheyne, who would later be Broyles' sports information director at Arkansas. "John Barnhill, the Arkansas athletic director, was well aware of how brilliant Frank was. That's why he hired him as head coach several years later."

Georgia Tech won six consecutive bowl games while Broyles was there. Finally, Broyles made the leap to head coaching and left for Missouri prior to the 1957 season. A year later he was hired as head coach at Arkansas.

In Broyles' second season at Fayetteville, the Razorbacks finished 8–2 and shared the Southwest Conference championship. The Hogs didn't secure the Cotton Bowl spot because of a one-point loss to co-champion Texas, who won the tiebreaker. There was still a great reward, though. Arkansas was paired with Georgia Tech and Broyles' mentor, Bobby Dodd, in the Gator Bowl.

"I don't know what Frank told the team, but he tried to not make a big deal about it with the press," Cheyne said. "That didn't keep the media from making it a matchup of Bobby Dodd and his former pupil and assistant Frank Broyles. I'm sure the players made a big deal about it, too. They felt like Broyles was *their* coach, not Georgia Tech's and they wanted to win the game for him."

The Razorbacks did just that. After spotting the Yellow Jackets a 7–0 lead, the Hogs tied it in the second quarter on a one-yard blast by Joe Paul Alberty, then took the lead on Jim Mooty's 19-yard touchdown sprint in the third quarter. Mooty finished with 99 rushing yards and the lead held up. Arkansas' 14-7 triumph snapped Georgia Tech's bowl winning streak that Broyles had helped construct and gave the coach his first-ever bowl win at head coach.

"That was a great moment for me and for our program," Broyles said. "It was our first bowl win and helped us build momentum for the great decade that followed. Coach Dodd was a fierce competitor, but was very gracious when the game was over."

While Broyles and Dodd never faced each other again (the Hogs and Yellow Jackets still haven't met since), there were those who believed Broyles would eventually go back to his alma mater as head coach when Dodd retired.

"When I came to Arkansas, I came to stay," Broyles said. "I didn't want anyone to use my name in regard to another coaching job to hurt us in recruiting. I asked Bob Cheyne to write a statement for me to use anytime my name came up."

Cheyne said, "I wrote a brief statement that said Frank was staying at Arkansas and not going to Georgia Tech, and he approved it. Any time a sportswriter would call to inquire about

Frank going to Georgia Tech or any place else, I would read that statement."

Indeed, Broyles stayed another 48 years as head coach, then as athletic director. But even all these years later, he still relishes that early victory against his former coach.

96 Kendall Trainor

Kendall Trainor grew up in the small community of Fredonia, Kansas. He had walked on as a kicker at the University of Arkansas in the fall of 1985. He hadn't even kicked any field goals yet when he was offered a scholarship on his third day as a Razorback. He had shown enough promise as a punter that coach Ken Hatfield was determined to keep him.

"We were stretching, and he asked me if I thought my parents would mind if I received a full scholarship," Trainor recalled. "We called them and they were thrilled."

Trainor indeed became the placekicker, starting as a freshman. He struggled a bit, mostly on longer attempts, but the Razorbacks finished the regular season with a 9–2 record and earned a spot against Arizona State in the Holiday Bowl.

"During our last practice before the game, Coach Hatfield told us to line up and we would try a last-second field goal to win the game," Trainor said. "I kicked it and thought I hit it pretty good but I heard two thumps. I looked up and my kick had hit the snapper, Richie Miller, in the rear. I had never done that before in my life. Everyone was stunned. Coach Hatfield said, 'Well, I guess we lost.'"

Wouldn't you know it, with less than 30 seconds left the Hogs trailed Arizona State 17–15 but were deep enough in Sun Devils territory to attempt a 37-yard field goal to win the game.

"It was the exact same distance as the one I had muffed in practice," Trainor said. "Arizona State called timeout and Coach Hatfield started telling me about a kicker he had at Air Force. He had a chance to beat Notre Dame with a field goal, but Notre Dame called two timeouts. Before he could finish the story, it was time to go out on the field.

"After I had missed the field goal in practice, Bob Carver [a car dealer who spotted for the radio network] started talking to me about fishing in order to relax me. For some reason, when I went on the field for that field goal attempt, I was thinking about fishing rather than the kick. The snap was perfect, the hold was perfect, and the kick went straight through the uprights.

"Arizona State actually had a 60 yard or so shot at a field goal even after our kick but missed. After the game in the dressing room I asked Coach Hatfield if his Air Force kicker made the field goal. He said no. I guess I'm glad he didn't finish the story before I tried the field goal."

Two years later Trainor had a chance to beat Georgia with a late field goal in the Liberty Bowl. He recalled, "It was the coldest I ever was as a player. My body never felt normal. I [had] missed another kick earlier. I missed wide left, then Georgia kicked a field goal on the last play of the game to beat us. It was sad in the locker room. Those of us who would be seniors the following year used it as a time to recommit ourselves to doing much better."

During the following preseason Trainor faced intense competition from freshman Todd Wright. The plan was to redshirt Wright, but when Trainor got off to a slow start, then missed a field goal and an extra point in the first half of the third game of the season against Ole Miss, his job was in jeopardy.

Kicking Tennessee

On the October 1992 morning of Arkansas' first SEC visit to Tennessee, *Knoxville Sentinel* columnist John Adams wrote that the Razorbacks should never have been invited to join the Southeastern Conference to begin with. He said the Hogs brought nothing to the table, and cited their opening game loss to the Citadel and 1–4 record, including lopsided losses to Alabama and Georgia.

Adams suggested the Razorbacks had no chance of beating the Volunteers—who were undefeated and ranked fourth nationally—that afternoon in Neyland Stadium. Whether or not any of the players read Adams' column, the Hogs showed themselves worthy of SEC stature.

With freshman quarterback Barry Lunney Jr. making his first varsity start, Arkansas led until the third quarter. Once the Vols started scoring, it looked as if they might pull away. Tennessee led 24–16 with less than three minutes left when it punted to Orlando Watters.

Using superb blocking, Watters sped 71 yards for a touchdown. Suddenly Vols fans weren't breathing so easily. Things looked better for the home team when the Hogs missed a two-point try.

However, Arkansas quickly recovered an onside kick, giving the Razorbacks one last shot to get into scoring position. But Lunney got sacked on second down, leaving the Hogs with third-and-18.

"We had a play called 'cube,'" said Houston Nutt, an assistant coach that year. "Greg Davis called it on that play. It was a high-low with Tracy Caldwell and Ron Dickerson Jr. Tracy was supposed to go 15 or 16 yards and Ron went underneath. Barry threw it perfectly and Tracy made the catch in full stride. We needed 18 yards and made 19."

Later in the drive Lunney called an audible on third-and-3 and hit Dickerson just before he went out of bounds for a first down. With three seconds left, Todd Wright went onto the field to try a 41-yard field goal.

"Todd was a freshman when I was a senior, and I knew he was meant to be a kicker," said Kendall Trainor. "He had the perfect demeanor. He never got too excited and never got depressed. His inner drive was tenacious. I was watching on television. When Tennessee called two timeouts, I knew Todd would make it."

Wright drilled it through the middle of the uprights for a 25–24 Razorback victory. Nutt said, "It had been a tough year with not much going right, but when Todd made that kick our sidelines went crazy, and 100,000 Tennessee fans went deathly silent."

The Hogs didn't stick around to see what John Adams wrote after the game.

"[Kickers] Coach [Ken] Turner walked by my locker when we came in at half time and muttered, 'All Trainor is is a choker.' I followed him to the coaches' locker room but he wouldn't stop. I went back to my locker and sulked. Coach Turner told me later the staff had discussed it at halftime and decided if I missed another field goal they were going to give Todd a chance.

"After I had sulked a while I stood on a chair and told everyone I wouldn't miss another field goal all season. That was my way of pumping myself up. Jim Mabry and Rick Apolskis, two of our starting linemen, just rolled their eyes. Later they told me they believed me, but I don't think so.

"When I went out for the second half, being superstitious as all baseball players are [he played baseball at Arkansas], I took my shoe off and threw it at the trashcan on the sideline. It hit the rim and rolled off. I heard this voice saying, 'Trainor, way to go. You were wide right again.' I looked up and it was my brother, Kevin. He was joking with me."

Trainor put on another shoe, kicked two field goals in the second half, and, true to his word, never missed another that season. His streak reached 24 in a row when he made a 58-yarder at Miami in the regular-season finale.

"I got a little lucky but there was a pretty good wind," Trainor said. "I hit one from 68 yards before the game and had several others longer than 60. In the first quarter Coach Hatfield asked me if I could make it. Being young and dumb I said yes. We set up eight yards deep rather than the normal seven. The snap and hold were perfect. The ball hit the upright and fell over the crossbar."

Trainor made one more field goal after that. It was against UCLA in the Cotton Bowl. It would have made 25 in a row, except that bowl game statistics didn't count on team or individual statistics during that time.

For his efforts Trainor earned all-America honors, then went on to a brief career in the pros. He even took to camp with the Cardinals the same shoe he wore to kick 25 in a row. "I used it until it fell apart," he said.

Trainor's consecutive-kick record still stands, even though there have been several great kickers since. Ish Ordonez kicked 16 in a row in 1979 before having one blocked. No one else has come close.

97 Broyles Athletic Center

Even though Arkansas is regarded as a southern state, it gets cold in the northwest corner, where the university is located. Early in his tenure as athletic director, and while still serving as head football coach, Frank Broyles decided the football team needed a place to practice no matter what the weather might be. At that time there was no such thing as an indoor practice area. Broyles built the first one. When it opened in 1975 it was the palace of its day.

"Late in the season we would frequently have days where outdoor practice conditions were horrible," Broyles said. "We raised the money to build an indoor facility that also would house our coaches and other administrators. South Carolina built an indoor practice facility at the same time, but theirs didn't have all the offices ours did."

The board of trustees voted to name it after Broyles, who was still head coach during the first two years the building was in use. He remained under its roof as athletic director for another 31 years.

The Broyles Center was the envy of schools all over the country. They came, studied, and built. By the time Arkansas entered the SEC in August 1990, the building was already in need of renovation. In 1993, the overhaul began. The building was almost totally gutted and put back together again. A museum was added. Dressing rooms were enlarged. So was the training room.

After a year in temporary quarters, coaches and administrators moved back in. The building was SEC competitive again. But in the arms race that is collegiate athletics, several schools quickly caught up to or surpassed the Broyles Center.

Timed to the beginning of the 2013 season, the Fred W. Smith Football Center was opened to house the Razorbacks football program. Administrators remained in the Broyles Center and were joined by several members of the staff that had been housed in Barnhill Arena.

With a statue of Broyles guarding the entrance, the Broyles Center still ranks as one of the great facilities in the country, especially considering football has a new home a short walk away.

98 Visit the Broyles Center Museum

Any Arkansas fan who hasn't visited the museum in the Broyles Athletic Center should do so. Originally opened in 1994, it is filled with artifacts, displays, and facts about Razorbacks football, much of it collected by Orville Henry, the longtime, legendary sportswriter who covered the Razorbacks for more than 50 years.

Henry may have been the only man in Arkansas who could have contacted so many former Razorbacks and their families and had so much success securing the treasures that appear in the Broyles Center. Henry somehow discovered a yearbook when Arkansas was the Cardinals. He found pictures of teams from the

Hugo Bezdek was the first big-time Razorbacks football coach, and is prominently featured at the exhibits in the Broyles Center Museum.

1920s and even earlier. He even came up with a UA pennant when the school color was a shade of purple.

"A lot of players put their blood, sweat, and tears in the program and they were very generous in helping us put the museum together," said Henry at the time of its opening.

There have been some renovations since Henry's initial effort, from new donations to updating for Razorbacks greats who followed. Most notably among the latter is a new a display on Darren McFadden, who was twice runner-up in the Heisman Trophy race.

It's Arkansas history on display and well worth your time.

99 World's Largest Scoreboard

Any Razorbacks football fan knows how gigantic the big-screen video board at Reynolds Razorback Stadium is. In fact, during games, it's hard to keep your eyes off of it and on the action on the field.

When Arkansas expanded Reynolds Razorback Stadium in time for the 2001 football season, athletic director Frank Broyles declared that he wanted the largest video screen scoreboard in the country. And for a brief period of time, he got his wish.

At the time of its installation, no stadium had ever seen a video board as large as the one installed above the Broyles Athletic Center in the north end zone. When it was first tested, its signal disturbed air traffic. Cars driving south on I-540 could see the screen as they neared the first Fayetteville exit.

"It was phenomenal," said Broyles. "Our fans were in awe. I had never seen anything like it, and neither had most of our fans. It not only was the biggest in the country, it was the best. The quality of the picture was unbelievable."

For the first season or two, many fans were so captivated by the screen that they followed the action by gazing up above the north end zone rather than watching it unfold on the field. Added to which, replays gave patrons a second and third look at the most spectacular Razorback plays. And even after the newness wore off and larger screens began to appear in other stadiums, Razorbacks fans loved the big picture that was delivered to them in the stadium.

Technology kept improving and Jeff Long, Broyles' successor as athletic director, had the video board updated before the 2012 season. Incredibly, the board's size was nearly doubled to 38 feet high by 167 feet wide. The high-definition picture was and is striking. It surpassed many of its competitors and became the second largest on-campus video display board in the country.

100 Razorback Foundation

When Frank Broyles became athletic director in 1973, he was faced with a mandate from Razorbacks fans. He was still head football coach and Arkansas football had prospered under his direction—but Hog fans wanted more.

"Everywhere I went fans told me they wanted an all-sports program," Broyles said. "They loved football and would always love football, but they wanted more than that. People would tell me they had a son who played baseball, golf, or tennis but they had to send them somewhere else because we just didn't offer much in those sports."

Broyles inherited an athletic budget of about $900,000, and football utilized more than 70 percent of that. That didn't leave much leftover.

"I assembled 300 business leaders from all over Arkansas at a meeting in Little Rock," Broyles recalled. "I told them we needed to raise money for an all-sports program. Not one of those businessmen hesitated. They all said they would support us."

In effect, that meeting was the birth of the Razorback Foundation. Broyles raised considerable dollars that day—but the fund-raising had to be sustained. Through his efforts, giving was promoted throughout the entire fan base. Eventually seats at Razorback Stadium and War Memorial Stadium were tied to contributions.

"We never moved anyone," Broyles said, "but we encouraged them to give. We wanted them to give because they loved the Razorbacks, not to get better seats. Obviously, if someone was new to the program we wanted them to make a contribution in order to buy seats."

Broyles handed the fund-raising duties to Wilson Matthews, the legendary former Little Rock Central High School football coach who had served faithfully as an assistant on Broyles' staff. Matthews had taken on administrative duties a couple years earlier and was perfect for the position.

Matthews fielded complaints from season-ticket holders like he did mistakes on the football field. By the time a ticket buyer was off the phone with Matthews, he would probably have pledged more money and have been convinced he was lucky to have tickets at all.

The Foundation officially incorporated and moved off campus in 1988. When Matthews retired, he was followed as president of the foundation by Terry Don Phillips, Chuck Dicus, and Harold Horton, all former Razorbacks players.

Monies contributed to the Razorback Foundation have been used for decades for improvements to the athletic facilities. A huge chunk went to the expansion and renovation of Razorback Stadium. Current and future funds will help construct the indoor baseball practice space and track facility, a basketball practice facility, and an academic center.

Sean Rochelle is the current president of the Razorback Foundation. At one time he served in the academic service wing of the athletic department. Broyles and Horton still have emeritus status. Former Razorbacks baseball coach Norm DeBriyn, former trainer Dean Weber, and former Hog football player Marvin Caston are also on the staff.

Acknowledgements

Before acknowledging anyone else I always must thank my wife, Adelaide, my son, Benny, and his best friend Eddie, for their patience in allowing me to work weekends and nights to complete this project. I sincerely appreciate their sacrifice, as well as the times when Adelaide cheered me on as I neared completion.

I hesitate to thank all the former and current Razorbacks who shared their stories for fear of leaving someone out, but special thanks go to Frank Broyles, Jeff Long, Quinn Grovey—whose comments in the foreword were extraordinarily generous—Ron Brewer, Joe Ferguson, Ken Hatfield, Houston Nutt, Mike Anderson, Chuck Barrett, Mike Nail, Kendall Trainor, Todd Day, Lee Mayberry, Harold Horton, Scotty Thurman, Tim Horton, Muskie Harris, Bill Burnett, Jay Bequette, Dennis Winston, Jarius Wright, Ryan Mallett, Zach Hocker, Dean Weber, U.S. Reed, and particularly Bob Cheyne.

I visited Bob Cheyne, who was sports information director at Arkansas from 1948 to 1968 and voice of the Razorbacks from 1958 to 1967, five weeks before he passed away. He was fantastic. His memory was tremendous, and he shared enormous insights that helped make this a more complete work. I never suspected it would be the last time I would see him.

Others who deserve thanks include all the former Hogs who visited with me for the first book I wrote, *The Game of My Life: Memorable Stories of Razorback Football.* Thank goodness I saved all my notes from that one.

Mary Lynn Gibson, who has been with the sports information staff at Arkansas since my time there, was very helpful in providing past press guides and game summaries. Thanks to the entire SID staff for always being so helpful.

Thanks also to Long, UA athletic director, and David Shoemaker of Razorback Sports Properties (IMG) who continue to allow me to participate in the broadcasts of Razorbacks football, basketball, and baseball games. It is a privilege I never take lightly or for granted.

Special thanks to Dr. Jim Rollins, superintendent of Springdale schools, who allows me the privilege of serving as his Communications Director and remaining connected to Razorback Athletics.

Finally, thanks to Tommy and Cathy DeWeese for allowing me access to Bob Cheyne's photo collection. Cathy is Bob's daughter.

Sources

The Razorbacks: A Story of Arkansas Football by Orville Henry and
    Jim Bailey

The Game of My Life: Memorable Stories of Razorback Football by
    Rick Schaeffer

Football Media Guides, University of Arkansas

Basketball Media Guides, University of Arkansas